Merry Ch[ristmas]
Thank [you for all]
you do to help others!
So grateful!
xoxo
Jenn

BUBBLY

BUBBLY

A COLLECTION OF CHAMPAGNE
AND SPARKLING COCKTAILS

COLLEEN JEFFERS

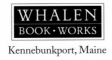

WHALEN
BOOK·WORKS

Kennebunkport, Maine

Bubbly

Copyright © 2019 by Whalen Book Works LLC.

This is an officially licensed book by Whalen Book Works LLC.

13-digit ISBN: 978-1-73251-265-8
10-digit ISBN: 1-73251-265-5

This book may be ordered by mail from the publisher. Please include $5.99 for postage and handling. Please support your local bookseller first!

Books published by Whalen Book Works are available at special discounts when purchased in bulk. For more information, please email us at info@whalenbookworks.com.

Whalen Book Works
68 North Street
Kennebunkport, ME 04046

whalenbookworks.com

Cover and interior design by Melissa Gerber
Photography by Colleen Jeffers
Food and prop styling by Colleen Jeffers
Typography: Gotham, Adobe Caslon, and Eveleth Clean Thin

Printed in China
6 7 8 9

For Pat

Hibiscus Fizz (page 124)

CONTENTS

INTRODUCTION

Rosemary-Chartreuse Spritz (page 58)

AUTHOR'S NOTE

I didn't come by my cocktail knowledge in the usual way: behind the stick, tending bar. There are many books surrounding this one on the shelf written by people who did, and I encourage you to read them. I've personally benefited from the willingness of pioneers to share their hard-earned experience in ways I can't begin to describe.

My experience comes from making cocktails at home. I drink them curled up on couches or chatting over the kitchen counter. I serve them on decks and porches, beaches and backyards, at holiday parties and weekend getaways. I feel that these moments are as worthy of a good drink as any on a barstool.

I know the limitations of an average kitchen, an average liquor store, and an average budget because I've been working under them for years. I won't ask you to make a homemade syrup you won't use twice. I'll let you know just how expensive Chartreuse is before I ask you to buy it. I stuck to two types of bitters when I wanted to involve a third, and one orange liqueur when I wanted to use two. If you can skip a step in a bind, I'll let you know.

There aren't hundreds of recipes in this book, because each one had to earn its place in your kitchen, the kitchen of a stranger who's welcomed me in. I don't take your precious leisure time—your seasons and gatherings and free moments—lightly. The cost and effort I'll ask you to spend on any one step or ingredient must be justified by a proportionate gain in flavor. I promise you that none of these drinks are dull, and that your loved ones will love them. I promise that I've described the absolute best way to make each drink without compromise, but also the simplest way to do so.

The dry practicality that went into the development of these recipes found balance in the pure joy of dreaming them up and of imagining you enjoying each one. I pictured you in your own kitchens and couches and beaches and backyards, experiencing the pure bliss that is a perfectly mixed drink. I hope that you'll return to these pages whenever you're in need of that bliss, over and over again.

—*Colleen Jeffers*

PICK YOUR POISON: BUYING THE RIGHT CHAMPAGNE FOR COCKTAILS

You have this book, so you're ready to try a champagne recipe. You make your way to the wine store and find the sparkling section. You're face to face with a (hopefully large) wall of choices—do you want to buy Champagne from France, or a Blanc de Blancs from Oregon? Should it be labeled "Brut," "Dry," or "Doux"? Do you need to shell out a small fortune, or are any of those bottles under $20 worth taking home with you?

When your sparkling wine is destined for a cocktail, you're looking for a bottle with a Goldilocks fit—not so fine that the nuances are wasted on the drink, and not so inferior that it spoils the whole. In a word? You want to use wine that's good. Just good—not *too* good.

You won't see champagne with a capital "C" called for in any of these recipes. That's because, generally speaking, a wine should only be capitalized when it's named for a place and actually comes from that place. In other words, Champagne with a capital "C" must come from the Champagne region of France (in fact, true Champagne must also be made in accordance with a strict method laid out by the Appellation d'Origine Controlée). Though you're welcome to use true Champagne in these recipes—some, like Pol Roger, are sold at a less prohibitive price point—you certainly don't need to.

When a style of wine is named for a place but doesn't actually come from that place, we don't capitalize it. So when I refer to chilled champagne in most of these recipes, I'm simply calling for any dry, sparkling wine. When I call for a specific sparkling wine—prosecco, for example—it's because that type has something specific to contribute to the recipe (i.e., melon notes that work well with honeydew).

If you don't already have access to an affordable favorite (say you live in a domestic wine-growing region like California and really love Roederer wines), I recommend that you use cava for most of these recipes. Cava is a

Spanish sparkling wine made using the same general production method as Champagne, with different grapes and a bit less time aging. The advantage? Most cava costs $20 or less, making it one of the most affordable sparkling wines on the market with fairly consistent quality. And unlike some other alternatives, I can find it almost everywhere.

Now, if you thought the capitalization of champagne was a bit overcomplicated, let's move on to the head-scratching titles used to designate sweetness. Not everyone pays attention to terms like "Brut" on a label, but they're actually pretty crucial to understand if you don't want to end up with a dessert wine when looking for something bone-dry. The sugar content of sparkling wines is usually categorized under the following terms:

— **Extra Brut** — Dry (or Sec)
— **Brut** — Semi-Dry (or Demi-Sec)
— **Extra Dry (or Extra Sec)** — Doux

Now, which of those might we assume is the driest? Perhaps the so-called Extra Dry? Believe it or not, both Brut and Extra Brut are *drier* than Extra Dry. Take another look at the list—I've ordered these terms from driest to sweetest, meaning that wines labeled "Dry" are actually on the sweeter side of the spectrum. Every time I walk into a wine store and see a semisweet sparkling wine with a big, bold "Dry" on the label, I shake my head a little at the confusion these categories are causing.

For the recipes in this book, you'll want to purchase wines in the Brut category. These wines are pleasantly dry, which means we have better control over the sweetness of the finished drink (no unexpected sugars to factor into the recipe).

A final tip: many champagne cocktails don't call for much champagne at all, which means you can get away with buying a half or "split" bottle instead. Take a look at the recipe, decide how many servings you'll need, and then multiply the recommended amount of champagne (often just 1 or 2 ounces) by that number. If it's under 12 ounces, you can opt for the 375-milliliter half bottle.

TLDR

(Too long, didn't read?)
Here are the takeaways:

• You don't need to buy authentic
Champagne for cocktails.

• Cava is your best option for good
quality at a reasonable price.

• Use prosecco, rosé, or lambrusco
(all affordable) when called for specifically.

• Buy wines labeled "Brut," not
"Dry" or "Extra Dry."

• Many champagne cocktails don't
call for much champagne, so a
half bottle will suffice.

UNDERSTANDING CARBONATION: HOW TO KEEP THINGS BUBBLY

If you really want to understand the science behind champagne carbonation, you'll need to read an entire book on the subject (I've recommended my favorite in Resources, page 166). But this short primer will help to shed light on some of the methods laid out in the recipes here.

Effervescence isn't just a festive look for a wine, or a pleasant feeling in your mouth. It dramatically affects the flavor and aroma of any carbonated liquid. CO_2, the gas present in sparkling wines, has an actual taste. It's difficult to describe—sharp, biting, in the sour family but not acidic. The amount of CO_2 in a drink determines just how much of that flavor you'll get. In other words, it behaves just like any other ingredient (more is more, less is less), so we need to control the amount present to achieve consistent flavor.

The problem is that CO_2 doesn't want to stay put in your glass—it wants to escape. Imagine if the sugar in your cookies started to dissolve into thin air the moment you took them out of the oven. You'd eat them pretty quickly, right? This is the challenge of carbonated cocktails—keeping the CO_2 in the glass long enough for you to enjoy them.

Carbonation has many enemies (for example, the amount of alcohol or protein in the drink), and you can't control them all when you're following a set recipe. The major factors you *can* control when you're using this book are (1) temperature, (2) foaming, and (3) the surface area of the drink.

(1) VERY SIMPLY PUT, HEAT IS TERRIBLE FOR STABLE CARBONATION. You want your glassware and ingredients to be as cold as you can get them to be. The colder the liquid, the more CO_2 it can hold, and the less carbonation you'll lose. Store your ingredients—champagne included—in the coldest section of your refrigerator, and chill glasses in the freezer. I store a selection of champagne coupes and flutes in my freezer permanently, but you don't need to go that far. Just place the glasses you're using in the freezer as you start to assemble the drink.

(2) FOAMING, OR RAPID BUBBLING, IS ANOTHER GREAT ADVERSARY OF CARBONATED DRINKS. CO_2 needs something known as a nucleation site to escape your drink in the form of bubbles. These nucleation sites can be anything in or touching the liquid—an ice cube, a scratch on your glass, even the suspended particles in a fruit juice. You can reduce foaming by straining as finely as possible whenever called for (a fine mesh strainer is most convenient, but cheesecloth or nut milk bags are actually best), using clean glassware free of scratches (even a bit of lint in the glass can become a nucleation point), and by pouring slowly and carefully at an angle—tilt your glass 45 degrees, and slowly raise the glass to vertical as you pour.

(3) THE OTHER WAY FOR CO_2 TO ESCAPE YOUR DRINK IS THROUGH ITS SURFACE. Smaller surface areas lead to less carbonation loss. This is controlled by the type of glassware you use, and how high you pour the drink. Traditional flutes with small openings hold carbonation best, as do higher pours (you get more volume for the same surface area). You should always pour high, meaning you want to use as small a glass or flute as possible for the finished volume of the drink (so many coupes and flutes on the market nowadays are positively massive). But I don't always use a flute, as you can see throughout this book. The smaller opening of a flute makes it harder to perceive aroma, an important component of flavor. My personal rule of thumb is that if the drink will be consumed relatively quickly, I can go with a coupe or alternate glassware. If I feel that my guests might be nursing their drinks, I opt for the flute.

There's another major hurdle related to point number (2) that needs to be discussed at length. Measuring carbonated liquids (like the correct amount of champagne for each recipe) in any cup or jigger causes too much carbonation loss. This means you'll have to free pour, or eyeball it, a practice I generally despise and never advocate otherwise—it's way too easy to throw off the balance of a cocktail this way.

There are two ways to free pour with a greater measure of accuracy—by learning your glassware or by practicing in a measuring cup.

The first method is more accurate but can also be tricky, because you need to know the finished volume of your drink. This requires some calculation: the sum of the liquid ingredients, plus any added dilution for shaken (about 2 ounces) and stirred (about 1½ ounces) cocktails. If you have an accurate volume, you can measure that amount of water into the glass beforehand, and note the location of the "wash line," or water level. When it's time to top with champagne, pour it to that line.

The second method is a little easier to handle. Before you start mixing, practice pouring into a measuring cup, and count how long it takes you to pour the amount at a consistent speed (this is made easier by the fact that you should be pouring very slowly anyway). Do this at least a few times to ensure greater accuracy (I pour at a rate of about 1 ounce per 3 slow Mississippis). The upside is that you or a friend now have practice champagne to sip on as you mix.

Finally, it's worth a mention that the rumors are true—champagne actually *does* get you intoxicated more quickly than a still wine (the same holds true for all carbonated drinks). The scientific reasoning behind this has to do with CO_2 speeding up the digestive process, but what you should know is simply that alcohol enters your bloodstream more quickly when carbonation is present. In other words, serve your guests responsibly.

At the end of the day, don't get *too* hung up on the details. Spritzes call for ice, positively crawling with nucleation points, and they happen to be some of the most popular sparkling cocktails in the world. The effects of a 1-ounce champagne top-off are largely relegated to stirring up aroma, and will inevitably wear off within minutes. As the saying goes, have the serenity to accept the things you can't change, the diligence to change the things you can, and the wisdom to know the difference.

TLDR

(Too long, didn't read?)
Here are the takeaways:

• Keep these drinks as cold as possible by chilling your glassware and ingredients.

• Strain liquids through a fine mesh strainer (or better yet, a fine mesh strainer lined with cheesecloth) whenever called for.

• Use clean glasses free of scratches. Make sure the glass isn't too big for the drink.

• Don't measure champagne in a jigger—get to know your own glassware and practice free pouring.

• Pour champagne slowly and carefully, at an angle (tilt your glass).

• Serve responsibly—CO_2 gets alcohol into your bloodstream more quickly, meaning intoxication happens more quickly. Pace yourself and your guests.

SMALL TIPS, BIG IMPACT: EASY CHANGES THAT MAKE ALL THE DIFFERENCE

If you're not already in the habit of using the methods below (or if you have a valid reason for bypassing them), go ahead and bookmark this page— come back and reference the tips here frequently, until they become second nature. Well-made cocktails are all about nailing the details, and each one of these suggestions will help you do just that.

CHILL YOUR GLASSWARE—it only takes a few minutes in the freezer to create a noticeable difference, especially if you put the glasses right in front of the freezer's fan. This doesn't take advance thought or planning, since most cocktails take that long to assemble. Simply put the glasses in the freezer as soon as you start making your drinks. Five minutes are adequate, 10 are ideal. This tip is especially important when effervescence is at play, since heat is an enemy of carbonation.

CHILL YOUR INGREDIENTS IN THE REFRIGERATOR OR FREEZER IF YOU WON'T BE SHAKING OR STIRRING THEM (many of the cocktails in this book don't require mixing). That means the champagne itself, along with any unmixed syrups or liqueurs. For a standard bottle, 4 hours in the coldest part of your refrigerator (generally near a fan) or 1 in the freezer is satisfactory. Since I make a lot of spritzes, I simply keep my liqueurs in the fridge at all times.

SQUEEZE YOUR OWN CITRUS JUICE FROM FRESH PRODUCE AND STRAIN IT through a fine mesh sieve to remove bitter, foam-inducing pulp. Never, ever, ever use plastic squeeze bottles of lemon or lime juice in a cocktail. Juicing citrus in front of guests can be messy and time-consuming, so I usually prep mine beforehand. Due to the volatile acids in lemon and lime juice, it's best to squeeze and strain them only a few hours in advance. Oranges and grapefruits are more forgiving and can be juiced a full day ahead of serving. Store the strained juice in the refrigerator until ready for use, in a sealed container that's as small as possible in order to reduce "headspace," or the amount of air interacting with the liquid.

NEVER EYEBALL, ALWAYS MEASURE, AND USE ACCURATE EQUIPMENT (see the next section on tools). That souvenir shot glass gathering dust in the back of your cabinet doesn't count. If you have no real jigger (I run into this problem at friends' houses all the time, which is why I try to keep a good jigger in my purse), you're better off using a measuring glass (¼ cup = 2 ounces) for larger measurements and a tablespoon (1 tablespoon = ½ ounce) for smaller ones. Just make sure that if you're using two different cups or spoons for one recipe, you test them to make sure they really have the advertised capacities—you'd be shocked at how many tablespoons I've tested that don't actually hold a half ounce. If you're using one vessel consistently for all ingredients, this won't matter, because all the skewed measurements will still be in the proper ratio.

FOR EFFERVESCENT COCKTAILS LIKE THE ONES IN THIS BOOK, MAKE SURE YOUR GLASSWARE IS SMOOTH AND CLEAN. Scratches, chips, and even towel lint can deplete carbonation by providing nucleation sites—i.e., escape routes—for your precious CO_2. Aside from the loss of flavor, these nucleation sites will also cause unpleasant foaming while pouring.

TOOLS:
THE ONES YOU KNEW YOU NEEDED, PLUS SOME YOU DIDN'T

The basic tools of cocktail making are fairly well known, and you likely already have some or all of them. But for the sake of thoroughness, here's a tight list of essentials:

— Shaker

— Strainer

— Bar spoon

— Peeler for citrus twists

— Accurate jigger (measuring tool)

— Muddler

Instead of weighing in on the pros and cons of the tools above, a topic which has been covered at length by all the great cocktail authorities, let me refer you to one source instead: Cocktail Kingdom (see Resources, page 166). If you're missing any item on this list and need to purchase one, buy it there—any option you chose will be optimized for proper mixing. So many other sources sell tools that are beautiful, but not truly functional. If you don't understand the science and technique behind each tool, play it safe and get your stuff where they know what they're doing.

Now that we've covered the basics, we can move on to the other tools I use most frequently, many of them kitchen items that don't intuitively seem like bar essentials:

Kitchen scale: They're cheap. Your grocery store probably carries one in the kitchen tools section. And they're the best way to make almost every syrup. Most homemade syrups represent some combination of sugar and water—often equal parts. Since sugar and water have different densities, you can't accurately measure equal parts using the same measuring cup. The only way to make sure you're using the correct amount of both is to weigh them. Ditto for honey.

High-speed blender: I know, I know. They're expensive, and you've heard it all before. But having a Vitamix (or competing high-speed blender) really does make a world of difference, especially for cocktail making. More efficient blending means less air whipped into the liquid (oxygen is usually an enemy of freshness, particularly for delicate herbs and fruits) and smoother frozen drinks (not a factor in these recipes, but something to consider for general home cocktail making). Making simple syrup in a high-speed blender takes seconds—once you make a blender syrup, you'll never want to make one any other way.

Sous vide precision cooker: Surprisingly affordable for such a fancy-sounding tool (Anova makes a model under $100), a precision cooker will make you feel like a culinary prodigy without much real effort—using one is way easier than using a stove. For cocktails, a precision cooker enables you to infuse delicate ingredients into liquids at a very low heat, without any effects from evaporation or oxidation. I make many of my seasonal syrups this way, or more precise alcohol infusions in a fraction of the usual time.

Mini measuring beaker set (preferably from OXO): I don't measure my drinks with beautiful, classic metal jiggers. I use this set of beakers from OXO because they're simply the most accurate tools on the consumer market for measuring small volumes. What you gain in functionality, you lose in style—the color scheme is decidedly juvenile. But since I'm mixing drinks at home, not at a bar, I'm often in the kitchen out of sight, and I'll always choose precision over appearances when there's a notable advantage, as there is here. When you measure using a typical cone-shaped jigger, even a millimeter can represent a significant difference, to say nothing of the fact that most users don't fill all the way to the top because of spillage and difficulty pouring. I find these beakers so genuinely useful that I travel with them.

Medicine/eyedropper: Orange blossom water and rosewater appear in some of the recipes in this book, usually only a few drops at a time. Use a medicine or eyedropper to measure accurately—every drugstore should have one for only a few bucks. Also useful for bitters art, if you're into that sort of thing.

Citrus press: Use a press, not a reamer, when juicing citrus, to avoid unpleasant flavors from the bitter pith (which you're essentially muddling into the liquid when you ream). A handheld swing handle press is best for small citrus like lemons and limes, but I also have a countertop lever-pull press for larger fruit like oranges, grapefruits, and even pomegranates.

King cube ice tray: Extra-large, 2-inch ice cubes (commonly referred to as "king cubes") melt more slowly than regular cubes, giving them a distinct advantage in recipes that suffer when over-diluted. Get a standard tray for under $10 at most big-box stores, or splurge on a clear ice version (such as the trays made by True Cube or Wintersmiths).

Small and large fine mesh strainers: The smaller of my two fine mesh strainers sits comfortably over a measuring cup. Purchase one with a conical shape rather than the standard bowl shape—it will strain more quickly. I also have a large fine mesh strainer that sits over a mixing bowl. It comes in handy when juicing produce via the blender/strainer method (such as the watermelon and peach juices used in this book) or when straining higher-volume syrups and infusions.

Funnels and swing-top bottles: You just made yourself a homemade seasonal syrup or infusion. Congrats! Now where are you going to put it? Tupperware and mason jars are hard to pour from in small amounts, and a splash of sticky syrup on your floor or countertop is never any fun. Have a funnel and a few swing-top bottles in various sizes on hand to store your leftover liquids.

TO GARNISH, OR NOT TO GARNISH: A PHILOSOPHY

The garnish is a hotly debated element of the modern cocktail (if this statement seems a tad overblown, you probably don't run with a lot of cocktail nerds). On one hand, a perfectly mixed drink is a delicate thing, and plopping an unwieldy garnish on top of your masterpiece can sometimes mean "gilding the lily," or dressing up something that's already perfect as is. Even worse, a garnish that's too big, not fresh, or awkwardly placed can actually detract from the drinking experience.

On the other hand, we eat with our eyes. When it comes to cocktails, the garnish is the first way to show someone how much care we've put into a drink, how fresh the ingredients are, and what it will taste like. For example, the ever present pre-cut lime wedge that gets dunked into a Gin and Tonic at dive bars the world over says, "I made this drink quickly"—it doesn't signal thoughtfulness or freshness. But a bar that sends out its Old-Fashioned with a perfectly manicured strip of orange zest, peeled to order, without a spot of pith, is showing you that they care about every element of flavor going into that glass. When I order a drink and it comes to me with a sad garnish, I know not to expect much. An exceptional garnish tells me that I'm about to drink something exceptional.

So, how do you make sure your garnish is truly exceptional and not just getting in the way of your cocktail? Taste and aroma are the ultimate concern, but I would argue that beauty matters, too. An edible flower is simply gorgeous to look at, even when it's not adding aroma. It's signaling that you care enough about your cocktails to track down edible flowers, so the drinker can expect a carefully composed drink. And it's declaring that the moment is special, to be savored—put out a tray of nondescript drinks at a party next to a tray of beautifully garnished ones, and you know which one is going to go faster.

Here are my best practices when it comes to garnishing:

CONSIDER AROMA FIRST. Adding aroma to the glass in the form of a garnish is like adding another ingredient to the drink, since smell and taste are so closely related.

TELL A VISUAL STORY. If you want the drinker to feel beach-vacation vibes when sipping a cocktail, pineapple leaves might just be your ticket. Dark maraschino cherries are classic and refined. Nothing looks more refreshing than a slice of citrus, and a sprig of rosemary can signal a garden-fresh seasonality.

MAKE SURE THE GARNISH ISN'T ARRANGED IN SUCH A WAY THAT TAKING A SIP BECOMES AWKWARD. For example, if the garnish isn't meant to be eaten, it shouldn't be balanced precariously on the rim, waiting to fall off the moment you tilt your glass.

EFFERVESCENT COCKTAILS PRESENT A SPECIAL CHALLENGE IN THE FORM OF CARBONATION— anything dropped directly into the glass will rapidly deplete the cocktail's CO_2, an important element of its flavor. Don't let that prohibit you from garnishing. If the drink will be consumed fairly quickly, for example, the depletion won't be noticeable enough to matter. If the garnish is sturdy enough to stay firmly on the rim, go right ahead and balance it there. If there's ice in the drink, place the garnish on top.

I've suggested a garnish for most of the cocktails in this book according to these principles, but innovation and personalization are highly encouraged. The freshest ingredients will always have the best aroma, so sometimes a walk to the farmer's market or through your own garden will present an unforeseen opportunity. Have at it! Even the farthest reaches of your spice cabinet can be mined for inspiration. Try bay leaf, star anise, cinnamon sticks, vanilla beans, juniper berries, allspice, dried rosebuds, and peppercorns.

MASTER LIST: TWO-INGREDIENT COCKTAILS IN THIS BOOK

There will be occasions in life when you don't have time to assemble ingredients. Before you default to the usual beer and wine, know that you still have options. There are plenty of two-ingredient cocktails out there that look and taste more sophisticated than a Rum and Coke, for about the same amount of effort. These are the cocktails I sling on lazy summer evenings outdoors, or when friends stop by unannounced and my fridge is all but empty. They're what I'm drinking in moments of unexpected relaxation or spontaneity—in other words, some of life's best times.

Champagne as an ingredient is particularly suited to the two-ingredient cocktail category, because it brings acidity to the table in the form of tartaric and lactic acid, as well as the sharp, nearly-but-not-quite acidic flavor of carbonation. Which means you're already halfway to the sugar/acid balance that augments most great cocktails, without even squeezing a lime.

Kir Royale (page 40)	**Vermouth Spritz (page 64)**
Aperol Spritz (page 57)	**Bellini (page 90)**
Campari Spritz (page 52)	**Black Velvet (page 133)**
Elderflower Spritz (page 62)	**Sorbet Float (page 128)**
Lillet Spritz (page 66)	

I didn't count garnishes within the two ingredients for this list, because you don't have to include them. I didn't count the seltzer in a Campari or Aperol spritz, because you don't have to include that either. But since all of these recipes couldn't be any simpler, a strong garnish will have more impact (particularly within the spritz category). A citrus peel, a sprig of herbs, an edible flower—anything fresh and fragrant you have on hand is worth a try. If the drink includes ice, drop it right in. If it's served up, balance it on the rim.

Elderflower Spritz (page 62)

CHAPTER 1: CLASSICS

A CLASSIC BY ANY OTHER NAME

Cocktail history is a murky business. Sometimes we date a cocktail's age to the first time it appeared in print—maybe a recipe book, or a passing reference in a newspaper. But a cocktail well known enough to be published at all was likely around well before its first mention. Sometimes we consider a drink's place of origin to be the first bar to put it on a menu. But other times, we laud the bar that popularized the drink, serving it to enough patrons for it to become widely recognized. And if the two are different, who gets the real credit?

Mimosas were a vague but longstanding tradition in French wine country before they first made it into print in 1934, in *The Artistry Of Mixing Drinks* by Fred Meier. Many accredit the recipe to the author, but he himself did not—Meier initialed all of his original cocktails in the book, and the mimosa saw no such distinction. In any case, the drink was all but absent from the American drinking scene until the 1960s, after it became known in the media as the British royal family's favorite predinner cocktail. So, whom do we have to thank for the fact that every bartender in this country can serve a mimosa, and for its absolute omnipresence at brunch? Is it France at large, Fred Meier, or the Queen?

Quite a complicated backstory for a two-ingredient drink.

Origin stories are frequently fabricated and later debunked (see the **Seelbach**, page 35). Many times, we have not the slightest clue where or when a cocktail came to be. And what makes a classic cocktail "classic," anyway? Is it just age, or enduring popularity? Every cocktail enthusiast must, at some point, come to terms with their own definition, and mine (for the purposes of this book, at least) is this: Every cocktail you see in the following chapter is well known enough that you can ask a good bartender to make one for you. You can google each one and find more than one source.

In the long run, it's better that many, even most, of these storied drinks are more the stuff of legend than law. It makes adjusting them to your own palate a little more palatable.

CHAMPAGNE COCKTAIL

Tasting notes: bittersweet, crisp, aromatic, light baking spice

This classic cocktail is as simple as its name—just soak a sugar cube in bitters, top with bubbly, and watch it fizz. In fact, "watching it fizz" is kind of the point here. If we really just wanted to add a touch of bittersweet flavor to champagne, we would use a much more efficient sweetener: a syrup, which, unlike the sugar cube, is already dissolved. By opting for the rough-surfaced sugar cube instead, we're giving the CO_2 trapped in the wine hundreds of tiny nucleation points to bubble up from (see page 15 for more on the physics of fizz), creating an elegant little eruption inside the glass. Between the ease of the recipe and the spectacle it creates, the Champagne Cocktail is a perfect party drink.

YIELD: 1 COCKTAIL

---

1 demerara sugar cube

Angostura aromatic bitters

Chilled champagne, to top (about 5 ounces)

Optional: lemon twist, to garnish

(1) Place the demerara sugar cube on a small plate or bowl, then dash with the Angostura bitters until soaked.

(2) Place the soaked sugar cube in the bottom of a chilled champagne flute, then top slowly with the chilled champagne by pouring carefully and slowly down the side of the glass to reduce foam.

Optional: garnish with a lemon twist.

Note: *Serve in a tall flute, not a coupe, so the fizzing effect is more visible and lasts longer. As always, chill the glass beforehand and be careful when you pour—the bubbling on display here also exacerbates foaming.*

FRENCH 75

Tasting notes: tart, light, crisp, refreshing

Arguably the best known of all classic champagne cocktails, the French 75 also happens to be my favorite. Lightly acidic, floral, and effervescent, it's a study in balance—so much so that I used the basic format as a template for many of the seasonal recipes in this book. If you love the tart pop of fresh lemons, you may fall hard for this pale gold paragon. It's refreshing but elegant, vivacious but refined—the kind of cocktail that suits almost any occasion.

YIELD: 1 COCKTAIL

1½ ounces gin (such as Plymouth)

¾ ounce fresh, strained lemon juice

½ ounce Simple Syrup (page 164)

Chilled champagne, to top (about 2 ounces)

Optional: lemon twist, to garnish

(1) Combine the gin, lemon juice, and simple syrup in a cocktail shaker filled with ice. Shake hard for 15 seconds, then strain into a chilled champagne glass.

(2) Top with chilled champagne, by pouring carefully and slowly down the side of the glass to reduce foam.

Optional: garnish with a lemon twist.

Note: *Though gin is the most widely used spirit in the French 75 today, early versions of the cocktail used Cognac instead. If you'd like to try* **Cognac French 75**, *replace the gin in the recipe with 1 ounce of Cognac (I prefer Pierre Ferrand Ambre), and reduce the lemon juice to ½ ounce.*

Note: *For another variation, replace the 1½ ounces of gin with 1 ounce of bourbon to make a* **French 95**.

CHICAGO COCKTAIL

Tasting notes: boozy, bright with citrus and fruit

The Chicago Cocktail is one of those vintage drinks that tastes noticeably old-fashioned—you'll be transported to a speakeasy on first sip. The combination of brandies (Grand Marnier is a technically a brandy-based liqueur) makes for a profile that's both spirit and fruit forward, while a sugared rim adds a measure of sweetness to the equation. If you like a Brandy Crusta, you'll want to try this pared-down, fizzy cousin.

YIELD: 1 COCKTAIL

Lemon wedge and superfine sugar, for rim

1½ ounces brandy (such as Pierre Ferrand Ambre Cognac)

¼ ounce Grand Marnier orange-flavored liqueur

1 dash Angostura aromatic bitters

Chilled champagne, to top (about 1 ounce)

(1) Prepare the glass. Wet the rim of a chilled champagne glass with a cut lemon, then dip it lightly in superfine sugar to coat. Set aside.

(2) Fill a chilled mixing glass or metal shaking tin with ice, then pour the brandy, liqueur, and bitters into the vessel. Stir rapidly with a metal bar spoon for 15 seconds, then strain into the sugar-rimmed glass.

(3) Top carefully with chilled champagne.

Note: *Superfine sugar is a very fine granulated sugar popular behind bars for its ability to dissolve quickly. It's available in the baking section of most grocery stores, but if you can't find it, you can throw some regular granulated sugar in a blender or food processor, then blend until the crystals are slightly finer but not powdered.*

SEELBACH

Tasting notes: bitter, boozy, citrus, and vanilla

The history of this cocktail, purported to be a vintage creation from the Seelbach Hotel in Louisville, Kentucky, was later discovered to have been fabricated by Adam Seger, the hotel's bartender, in the 1990s—further proof that cocktail history is a tricky business. In any case, the notable component of this now well-known cocktail is its unusually high—14 dashes total—volume of bitters. If you love a bitter vermouth or amaro, give this whiskey-forward tipple a try.

YIELD: 1 COCKTAIL

1 ounce bourbon

½ ounce orange-flavored liqueur

7 dashes Angostura aromatic bitters

7 dashes Peychaud's aromatic bitters

Chilled champagne, to top (about 2 ounces)

Orange twist, to garnish

(1) Fill a chilled mixing glass or metal shaking tin with ice, then pour the bourbon, liqueur, and bitters into the vessel. Stir rapidly with a metal bar spoon for 15 seconds, then strain into a chilled champagne glass.

(2) Top carefully with chilled champagne, then express the orange peel by gently squeezing it, peel side down, over the surface of the drink. Swipe it around the rim, then drop it into the glass.

Note: *Since this drink falls vaguely into the Manhattan category (the made-up lore behind the drink included a Manhattan tie-in), you can choose to garnish it with an authentic maraschino cherry instead (see Note on* **Boothby Cocktail***, page 44).*

PRINCE OF WALES

Tasting notes: spirit forward, warm rye spice, tropical fruit

Queen Victoria's son, Albert Edward—Prince of Wales and later King Edward VII—embodied the stereotype of the fashionable playboy prince as he waited out his mother's reign for his own turn on the throne. A tastemaker in every sense, he's said to have created this cocktail himself. A heady mix of whiskey, bitters, and a touch of tropical sweetness topped off with crisp champagne, it certainly makes you feel *like royalty.*

YIELD: 1 COCKTAIL

1 pineapple cube
(about 1 inch)

1 lemon peel (about 1 inch
wide, 3 inches long)

1½ ounces rye whiskey

¼ ounce maraschino liqueur
(such as Luxardo)

¼ ounce Simple Syrup
(page 164)

1 dash Angostura
aromatic bitters

Chilled champagne,
to top (about 1 ounce)

Optional: pineapple leaves
and a slice, to garnish

(1) In the bottom of a cocktail shaker, muddle the pineapple cube and lemon peel with the rye, liqueur, syrup, and bitters.

(2) Add ice to the shaker, then shake hard for 15 seconds. Strain into a chilled champagne glass (or goblet).

(3) Top with chilled champagne.

Optional: garnish with pineapple leaves or a small slice of pineapple skewered on a cocktail pick.

Note: *Since maraschino liqueur is an ingredient here, feel free to garnish with a maraschino cherry as well (both preferably from Luxardo). And if you find yourself without access to pineapple, you can sub in a splash of pineapple juice instead. Mint also pairs well.*

NEGRONI SBAGLIATO

Tasting notes: bitter, botanical, complex, sharp, refreshing

Legend has it that this Negroni variation was born when a bartender accidentally added sparkling wine to the glass instead of gin. The "mistaken" Negroni (the Italian translation of sbagliato*) lives on as an effervescent version of the original, perfect as a bitter aperitivo (or predinner drink). Don't skip the orange peel—it adds a noticeable and necessary brightness to the cocktail that amplifies over time as you sip.*

YIELD: 1 COCKTAIL

1 ounce Campari

1 ounce sweet vermouth (such as Carpano Antica)

Chilled prosecco, to top (about 1 ounce)

Orange twist, to garnish

(1) In a rocks glass filled with ice (ideally one king cube), pour the Campari and sweet vermouth and stir until chilled, about 15 seconds.

(2) Top with chilled prosecco, then express the orange peel by gently squeezing it, peel side down, over the surface of the drink. Swipe it around the rim, then drop it into the glass.

Note: *If you're a fan of the bitter, bracing Negroni family, give the* **Campari Spritz** *(page 52) and* **Watermelon Campari Fizz** *(page 150) a try.*

Note: *For a standard citrus twist, use a sharp Y-shaped peeler to remove a wide strip of zest (about 3 inches long), then use a sharp knife to remove the bitter pith (the soft white part) from the back. Leaving the pith on will add unwanted bitterness to the drink. For a cleaner look, you can manicure the citrus peel by using a sharp paring knife to remove uneven edges. The flattened, angular look pictured here was achieved by simply removing all pith, then trimming the ends on a diagonal bias.*

KIR ROYALE

Tasting notes: refreshing, crisp, sour berry

A classic cocktail that couldn't be simpler—pour chilled black currant liqueur and champagne into a glass and call it a day. In addition to an appealingly deep plummy hue, the liqueur brings rich, tart berry notes to the table, which is perhaps why you see this cocktail return year after year for holiday toasts. Little effort, bold color, bright flavor. What's not to love?

YIELD: 1 COCKTAIL

½ **ounce chilled black currant liqueur (such as Clear Creek Distillery Cassis Liqueur)**

Chilled champagne, to top (about 5 ounces)

Optional: skewered maraschino cherry (such as Luxardo) or blackberries, to garnish

(1) Pour the chilled liqueur into the bottom of a champagne glass.

(2) Top with chilled champagne, by pouring carefully and slowly down the side of the glass to reduce foam.

Optional: garnish with a skewered maraschino cherry or blackberries.

Note: *The Kir Royale's reputation has been slightly marred by the proliferation of overly sweetened, bottom shelf "crème de cassis" liqueurs. The quality of this cocktail depends almost entirely on the quality of the liqueur, so make sure you're using an authentic black currant product. I like Clear Creek Distillery's Cassis Liqueur, but Lejay is another good option.*

CHAMPAGNE SIDECAR

Tasting notes: straightforward, citrusy, brandy sour

Another effervescent take on a classic, the Champagne Sidecar transforms the standard brandy sour into something at once more festive and refreshing. You'll notice deeper fall fruit notes from the Cognac (like apple and pear), and a more complex tartness that comes from merging the orange liqueur and lemon juice with champagne's tartaric and lactic acid. In other words, it opens the Sidecar up a bit to let each component sing.

YIELD: 1 COCKTAIL

---

1 ounce brandy
(such as Pierre Ferrand
Ambre Cognac)

1 ounce Grand Marnier
orange-flavored liqueur

½ ounce fresh, strained
lemon juice

Chilled champagne, to top
(about 1 ounce)

Optional: orange twist or
lemon wheel, to garnish

(1) Combine the brandy, liqueur, and lemon juice in a cocktail shaker filled with ice. Shake hard for 15 seconds, then strain into a chilled champagne glass.

(2) Top with chilled champagne.

Optional: garnish with an orange twist.

Note: *While in most cases any dry, sparkling wine will do, for this one I recommend a French bottle to go with the French brandy and liqueur. Just don't break the bank for something too nice, since you're only using about an ounce per drink—noticeable enough to put some care into your selection, but not so much that you'll be picking up on the subtler notes of a fine vintage.*

BOOTHBY COCKTAIL

Tasting notes: spirit forward, lightly bitter, caramel, vanilla, baking spice

Essentially a bourbon Manhattan with a champagne float, this drink will naturally appeal to the whiskey-inclined. Though cocktail history can be murky at best, it seems almost certain that this classic was named for legendary San Francisco bartender William T. Boothby. Smooth as velvet—dangerously so—with a touch of bitter baking spice, it feels very much like the special-occasion cocktail it's meant to be.

YIELD: 1 COCKTAIL

1 ounce bourbon

1 ounce sweet vermouth
(such as Carpano Antica)

2 dashes Angostura aromatic
bitters

Chilled champagne, to top
(about 1 ounce)

Optional: authentic
maraschino cherry (such as
Luxardo), to garnish

(1) Fill a chilled mixing glass or metal shaking tin with ice, then pour the bourbon, sweet vermouth, and bitters into the vessel. Stir rapidly with a metal bar spoon for 15 seconds, then strain into a chilled champagne glass.

(2) Top carefully with chilled champagne.

Optional: garnish with a maraschino cherry.

Note: *The candy red imitation "maraschino cherries" you see in Shirley Temples have no place in a grown-up drink. If you don't want to spring for real, Luxardo maraschino cherries (which retail around $19.99 a jar, but will last quite a while) or can't find them (try checking a well-stocked liquor store rather than a grocery store—or, of course, the internet), garnish with an orange twist instead.*

AIRMAIL

Tasting notes: bright, tropical fruit, honey, citrus, light rummy funk

The Airmail cocktail is another champagne sour (i.e., a combination of spirit, sugar, and citrus—close in profile to the French 75, but with a decidedly Caribbean bent. Lime replaces lemon, honey syrup replaces simple, and rum replaces gin, for a drink that will put palm trees and clear seas in mind. Although the origins of the Airmail's name are unclear, I like to think of it as a friendly postcard from an island vacation.

YIELD: 1 COCKTAIL

---

1 ounce aged Jamaican rum (such as Appleton Estate Signature)

½ ounce fresh, strained lime juice

½ ounce Honey Syrup (page 164)

Chilled champagne, to top (about 2 ounces)

(1) Combine the rum, lime juice, and honey syrup in a cocktail shaker filled with ice. Shake hard for 15 seconds, then strain into a chilled champagne glass.

(2) Top with chilled champagne, by pouring carefully and slowly down the side of the glass to reduce foam.

Note: *This cocktail is occasionally served over ice in a Collins glass. Try that version for outdoor or daytime affairs—it's decidedly more refreshing, with less bite. If serving over ice, use ¾ ounce honey syrup instead of ½ ounce, and serve with a lime wheel and straw.*

RITZ COCKTAIL

Tasting notes: spirit forward, bright, fruity, with citrus and light almond

Though one of the younger cocktails in this chapter, relatively speaking, this one has an established author: it was created by Dale DeGroff, a modern cocktail legend. Similar on first glance to the Champagne Sidecar, on the palette you'll immediately notice the addition of maraschino liqueur's fruity, nutty, indescribable funk.

YIELD: 1 COCKTAIL

¾ **ounce Cognac (such as Pierre Ferrand Ambre)**

½ **ounce orange-flavored liqueur**

¼ **ounce maraschino liqueur (such as Luxardo)**

¼ **ounce fresh, strained lemon juice**

Chilled champagne, to top (about 2 ounces)

Optional: Orange twist, to garnish

(1) Fill a chilled mixing glass or metal shaking tin with ice, then pour the Cognac, liqueurs, and lemon juice into the vessel. Stir rapidly with a metal bar spoon for 15 seconds, then strain into a chilled champagne glass.

(2) Top carefully with chilled champagne.

Optional: garnish with an orange twist.

Note: *Dale DeGroff actually calls for a flamed orange peel to garnish. I suggest YouTube if you want to learn this skill—some things are just beyond the ability of words to (safely!) describe.*

MOONWALK

Tasting notes: floral, citrusy, refreshing

The history of this cocktail is fairly well documented—it was created by Joe Gilmore, legendary Head Barman of the Savoy Hotel in London, to commemorate the 1969 lunar landing. Cocktail historians claim it as the first drink Neil Armstrong and Buzz Aldrin sipped after their return to earth (after waiting out their government-imposed quarantine, of course). In my opinion, it makes an excellent brunch cocktail.

YIELD: 1 COCKTAIL

---

1 ounce fresh, strained grapefruit juice

1 ounce Grand Marnier orange-flavored liqueur

3 drops rosewater

Chilled champagne, to top (about 2 ounces)

Optional: rose petal and grapefruit peel, to garnish

(1) Combine the grapefruit juice, liqueur, and rosewater in a cocktail shaker filled with ice. Shake hard for 15 seconds, then strain into a chilled champagne glass.

(2) Top with chilled champagne, by pouring carefully and slowly down the side of the glass to reduce foam.

Optional: garnish with a rose petal and peel.

Note: Rosewater is increasingly common in regular grocery stores—you'll likely find it in the international food section. And if you garnish with a rose petal, make sure to keep in mind that just because roses are edible doesn't mean that every bouquet is. Florists often treat the blooms with toxic chemicals, so make sure yours are organically grown for culinary purposes.

CHAPTER 2: SPRITZES

APERITIVO HOUR

The spritz is more a way of life than a category of drink. Entire books have been written on spritz culture, for good reason—it's a mind-set that should be spread. The spritz is meant to transition us from work to leisure. It's about taking a moment from the routine of daily life to catch up with friends, or to decompress before dinnertime, so we can actually enjoy the meal without fretting over an inbox. In our culture of rush and hurry, the spritz shifts focus from draining glasses and emptying plates to savoring the moment.

To that end, spritzes are low in alcohol, and served casually over ice. The point is relaxation, not intoxication. That way, if one aperitivo hour extends into a few, if the conversation is too good to leave or the sunset too beautiful, you can have more than one.

On a practical note, spritzes call for ice, an enemy of carbonation. For this reason, you'll want your ingredients to be extra cold (you're already losing CO_2 to massive nucleation sites—best not lose any to warmth as well). Don't use room-temperature liqueurs if you forgot to chill them in advance. Instead, alter the recipes so that you add the liqueur and ice first. Stir them rapidly for 20 seconds to chill, then top carefully with the carbonated ingredients.

CAMPARI SPRITZ

Tasting notes: bitter, bracing, citrus, and spice

A close relative of the Aperol Spritz—not quite twins, but definitely sisters—the Campari Spritz is more bitter, dry, and assertive. At 48 proof (to Aperol's 22), Campari is the bolder liqueur both in flavor and spirit, with its trademark crimson color and top-secret combination of bitter herbs and spices.

YIELD: 1 COCKTAIL

---

2 ounces chilled Campari

Chilled seltzer, (about 1 ounce)

Chilled prosecco, to top (about 3 ounces)

1 orange wedge or skewered green olives, to garnish

In a chilled wine glass, carefully pour the chilled Campari, chilled seltzer, and prosecco, in that order. Gently slide in ice and place the orange wedge or skewered green olives on top.

*Note: If you're a fan of the bitter Campari showcased here, try it in the **Negroni Sbagliato** (page 38) or the **Watermelon Campari Fizz** (page 150).*

SHERRY SPRITZ

Tasting notes: caramel oak, bright citrus, nuts, and dried fruit

The rich texture, nutty aroma, and tangy acidity of amontillado sherry is the star of the show in this all-season aperitivo. An effervescent lift from cava and a touch of bright citrus enliven the drink, which cries out to be served alongside a bowl of salty Marcona almonds or sliced Manchego cheese—ideally both.

YIELD: 1 COCKTAIL

---

1 ounce chilled amontillado sherry

1 ounce chilled Grand Marnier orange-flavored liqueur

Chilled cava, to top (about 3 ounces)

1 lemon wedge or wheel

In a chilled wine glass, carefully pour the chilled sherry, liqueur, and chilled cava, in that order. Gently slide in ice and place the lemon on top.

Note: In addition to the lemon peel, I often add green Castelvetrano olives (particularly when I'm serving the drink before dinner), or a bouquet of fresh mint (particularly when I'm serving the drink out of doors).

STRAWBERRY TARRAGON SPRITZ

Tasting notes: strawberry, anise, refreshing, fruity, herbaceous

A little bit of extra effort—slicing strawberries, letting them sit in a liqueur overnight—gains you a ton of fresh, juicy payoff in what has become my all-time favorite seasonal spritz. When strawberries are in season, beginning in spring and continuing throughout the summer, this is what you'll find in my hand during aperitivo hours.

YIELD: 4 COCKTAILS

---

6 strawberries, sliced thin

6 sprigs tarragon (about 4 inches long each)

1 cup liqueur of choice (such as Aperol, Campari, Lillet, or elderflower)

Chilled prosecco, to top (about 3 ounces per cocktail)

Optional: splash of good-quality balsamic vinegar and fresh sliced strawberries

(1) Combine the strawberries, tarragon, and liqueur in a sealed container and let sit at room temperature overnight, or 8 to 10 hours. Strain and store in the refrigerator (do not use until well chilled), reserving the infused strawberries for garnish.

(2) For each cocktail, pour 2 ounces of the infused liqueur into a chilled wine glass, then carefully top with the chilled prosecco. Gently slide in ice and sliced strawberries (reserved from the infusion, or fresh).

Optional: add a splash of balsamic vinegar and fresh sliced strawberries on top.

*Note: If you're not a fan of tarragon, this try this recipe with basil instead. For more on working with balsamic in cocktails, see A **Balsamic Garnish** (page 56).*

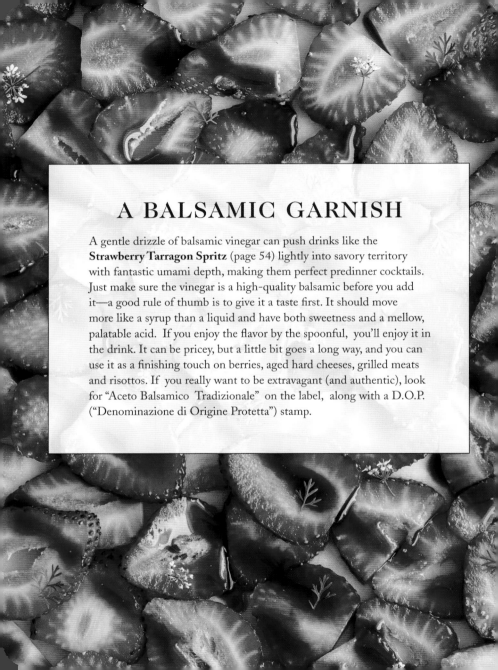

A BALSAMIC GARNISH

A gentle drizzle of balsamic vinegar can push drinks like the
Strawberry Tarragon Spritz (page 54) lightly into savory territory
with fantastic umami depth, making them perfect predinner cocktails.
Just make sure the vinegar is a high-quality balsamic before you add
it—a good rule of thumb is to give it a taste first. It should move
more like a syrup than a liquid and have both sweetness and a mellow,
palatable acid. If you enjoy the flavor by the spoonful, you'll enjoy it in
the drink. It can be pricey, but a little bit goes a long way, and you can
use it as a finishing touch on berries, aged hard cheeses, grilled meats
and risottos. If you really want to be extravagant (and authentic), look
for "Aceto Balsamico Tradizionale" on the label, along with a D.O.P.
("Denominazione di Origine Protetta") stamp.

APEROL SPRITZ

Tasting notes: bittersweet, refreshing, bright

No chapter on spritzes would be complete without the drink largely responsib for spreading spritz culture stateside: the iconic Aperol Spritz. A simple (and easy to remember) combination of 3-2-1 parts prosecco, Aperol, and seltzer, this low-alcohol cocktail is the ultimate aperitivo—a little bitter, a little sweet, and eminently relaxing.

YIELD: 1 COCKTAIL

---

2 ounces chilled Aperol

Chilled seltzer, to top (about 1 ounce)

Chilled prosecco, to top (about 3 ounces)

1 orange wedge or skewered green olives, to garnish

In a chilled wine glass, carefully pour the Aperol, seltzer, and prosecco, in that order. Gently slide in ice and place the orange wedge or skewered green olives on top.

Note: *Though I hate to mess with a cocktail so well known for its measurements, I don't think the drink suffers from cutting out the seltzer entirely if you don't have any on hand. Ice melt adds dilution to begin with, and the seltzer-less version is a lot easier to gather and assemble on, say, a beach.*

ROSEMARY CHARTREUSE SPRITZ

Tasting notes: bold, herbaceous, bright, refreshing

Green Chartreuse is a lot like Campari—it's not for everyone, but if you love it, you really love it. I make this spritz most frequently in the winter months, when the alpine flavors of the liqueur really shine, but its intense herbal punch is utterly refreshing in the heat of summer, too.

YIELD: 1 COCKTAIL

---

1 sprig rosemary

¾ ounce green Chartreuse

Chilled champagne, to top (about 3 ounces)

¼ ounce fresh, strained lime juice

(1) Rub the sprig of rosemary around the inside of a chilled wine glass, then set aside.

(2) Pour the Chartreuse, chilled champagne, and lime juice carefully into the glass, in that order. Gently slide in ice and place the rosemary sprig on top.

*Note: In the summer, mint in place of rosemary makes this spritz particularly cool and refreshing. For a **Mint Chartreuse Spritz**, use a few large sprigs of mint and swipe it gently around the inside of the glass—with mint's extremely delicate, volatile aromas, using more leaves allows you to handle the herb gently while still imparting noticeable flavor. Assemble the drink, and place additional mint on top of the ice.*

*Note: If you like the green Chartreuse in this spritz, give the **In Conclusion** (page 130) a try.*

HOPPED PINEAPPLE SPRITZ

Tasting notes: tropical, juicy, floral, refreshing

Beer, pineapple, and prosecco may seem like a strange combination, but try this easy summer shandy–spritz hybrid once and you'll instantly understand—it's pretty much liquid sunshine. I've seen many a non-beer-drinker go back for seconds (and thirds), since the beer's purpose is only to impart a light and refreshing floral hop bitterness, not to assert itself. Juicy and crisp, bright in color and flavor, it's tailor-made to quench your thirst and ramp up the vacation vibes.

YIELD: 1 COCKTAIL

Chilled prosecco
(about 2 ounces)

Chilled IPA beer
(about 2 ounces)

2 ounces chilled
pineapple juice

Optional: pineapple
leaves or slices,
maraschino cherries, or edible
flowers (such as dianthus)

In a chilled highball glass or tumbler, gently pour the chilled prosecco, the chilled IPA, and the chilled pineapple juice, in that order. Gently slide in ice and arrange pineapple leaves or slices, maraschino cherries, or edible flowers on top.

Note: *Try to pick a west-coast-style IPA that has strong floral and pine aromas—Simcoe, Centennial, Chinook, or Cascade hops are all a good start.*

Note: *Because this is an equal parts cocktail with a forgiving sense of balance, you can free pour everything without measuring—a little more or less of any single ingredient won't throw the whole thing out of whack. I'm often mixing this one outdoors (think concerts, tailgates, beaches, and barbecues), so it has to be no fuss.*

ELDERFLOWER SPRITZ

Tasting notes: light, refreshing, with bright fruit and floral notes

The bright, almost lychee–like flavor of the elderflower shines in this simple spritz, perfect for a spring afternoon. Layer in complexity with a grapefruit twist and sprig of rosemary—both are highly aromatic and lovely in the glass.

YIELD: 1 COCKTAIL

---

1 sprig rosemary

1 grapefruit twist

1½ ounces chilled elderflower liqueur

Chilled prosecco, to top (about 3 ounces)

(1) Rub the sprig of rosemary and the grapefruit twist around the inside of a chilled wine glass, then set them aside.

(2) Pour the chilled liqueur into the glass, then top carefully with the chilled prosecco. Gently slide in ice and place the rosemary and grapefruit twist on top.

*Note: If fresh lavender is in season, try a **Lavender Spritz**. You can replace the rosemary with a sprig of lavender for a more floral take (rosemary and lavender are actually close relatives with similar flavor profiles).*

VERMOUTH SPRITZ

Tasting notes: refreshing, lightly bitter, complex spice, bright acidity

This cocktail is a pick-your-own-journey sort of recipe, since much of the flavor comes from the vermouth, and you get to choose which one to use, along with an herb to garnish with. A red vermouth (like Carpano Antica) will be richer, lightly sweet, and more heavily spiced—I prefer it in winter, with rosemary, sage, or thyme. In the summer, white vermouth (also called "bianco" or "blanc," such as Dolin Blanc) plays well with mint, lemon balm, or shiso. This is a spritz, after all—the rules are flexible. When you choose your own preference, you can never be wrong.

YIELD: 1 COCKTAIL

---

1 sprig aromatic herb

1 lemon twist

1½ ounces chilled vermouth of choice

Chilled champagne, to top (about 3 ounces)

(1) Rub the aromatic herb and the lemon twist around the inside of a chilled wine glass or tumbler, then set them aside.

(2) Pour the chilled vermouth into the glass, then top carefully with the chilled champagne. Gently slide in ice and place the aromatic herb and lemon twist on top.

Note: This recipe seems the right place to note that vermouth absolutely must stay in the refrigerator once opened, ideally sealed with a vacuum stopper. Vermouth's reputation has been sullied over time by improper storage at bars and in homes—half-empty bottles sitting on shelves for months will oxidize and degrade just like a bottle of wine (though at a slower rate), developing unpleasant, vinegary acidity and all sorts of bad aromas. Even when stored properly in the fridge, vermouth should be consumed within a couple of months.

LILLET SPRITZ

Tasting notes: refreshing, light, gently fruity, delicately spiced

Like the Vermouth Spritz, this cocktail allows you to pick your own preference when it comes to Lillet: Blanc, Rouge, or Rosé. Blanc is perhaps the most refreshing, with bright acidity, fresh fruit, and gentle bitterness. Rouge drinks like a robust, fruity red wine, with a touch of bitter spice. Rosé (pictured here) is the most juicy and fruit forward, with a gentle sweetness perfect for pairing with a dry, sparkling rosé.

YIELD: 1 COCKTAIL

1½ ounces chilled Lillet of choice

Chilled sparkling rosé, to top (about 3 ounces)

Grapefruit segments and aromatics (like juniper berries, peppercorns, or fresh herbs), to garnish

Pour the chilled Lillet into the glass, then top carefully with the chilled sparkling rosé. Gently slide in ice and place the grapefruit segments and aromatics on top.

Note: Like vermouth, Lillet is an aromatized wine, which means it has to be stored in the same way—in the refrigerator, ideally with a vacuum stopper. When stored properly, it will retain great flavor for a couple or even a few months. It's great on its own, chilled, or over ice with a slice of citrus.

CHAPTER 3: PUNCHES

DRINKS FOR A CROWD

Punches are, in most cases, the easiest way to serve high volumes of guests. If you're hosting Thanksgiving this year, you won't be mixing drinks to order. I've made most of these recipes to accommodate 16 servings, which means a couple of rounds for 8 guests. Any of them can of course be doubled. I've been known to triple them for family parties (I come from a really big family).

You'll want to serve most of these punches over one large ice block. You can make these in any of your pans and containers (try putting the mold in the punch bowl before freezing to make sure it fits) and add fruits and flowers if you like. Tip: the block will be easiest to remove when it's just frozen through (especially handy for rigid molds). If you catch it at that phase, remove it right away, wrap it in plastic, and place it back in the freezer until ready for use. If you're really fancy, you can use a warm bread knife to slice away any cloudy parts for a perfectly clear block.

I chill my punch bowl and glasses in the freezer whenever possible. If the punch will be left sitting out unattended throughout a meal or party, don't bother. I like to assemble a punch just as guests are expected to arrive, then serve it in chilled glasses as soon as they walk in—that way, their first round, at least, is as cold (and carbonated) as possible.

PIMM'S PUNCH

Tasting notes: fruity, complex, lightly spiced, tart, refreshing

The Kentucky Derby has its julep, and Wimbledon has the Pimm's Cup—a tall, cool glass of summertime bliss. It's easy to see why this coupling of fruit and citrus, lightly woven through with aromatic spices, is the beverage of choice at outdoor sporting events (polo match, anyone?) in the United Kingdom. If you need to plan a party just to try this lively, refreshing punch, then so be it. Your patios and porches and decks are waiting.

YIELD: 16 SERVINGS

3 cups Pimm's Cup No. 1 Liqueur

1 cup gin (such as Plymouth)

2 cucumbers, thinly sliced

16 strawberries, thinly sliced (about 1 pint)

1½ cups Simple Syrup (page 164)

1 cup fresh, strained lemon juice (from about 6 lemons)

1 bottle sparkling rosé, chilled

Additional berry and cucumber slices, to garnish

(1) Combine the Pimm's, gin, cucumbers, and strawberries in a sealed container and let sit at room temperature overnight, or for 8 to 10 hours. Strain though a fine mesh sieve and store in the refrigerator. Use within 24 hours for best flavor.

(2) Pour the strained fruit infusion, simple syrup, and lemon juice into a punch bowl over one large ice block and stir rapidly until chilled (about 20 seconds). Add additional fruit slices to garnish, then top carefully with champagne and serve immediately.

Note: If you forget to infuse the gin and liqueur with the cucumbers and strawberries ahead of time, add them to the punch bowl when you assemble the punch, then ladle them into the glasses as you serve. You can even skip the strawberries and cucumbers altogether if you're really in a pinch—you'll lose all the fresh fruit flavor, but the drink will be still be well balanced, complex, and worth serving.

PALOMA PUNCH

Tasting notes: juicy grapefruit, tequila spice, crisp, tart, refreshing

One of Mexico's most beloved—and refreshing—cocktails, the sweet-tart Paloma is a true crowd-pleaser. So doesn't it just make sense to make enough for a crowd? A thirst-quenching combination of grapefruit and lime juices mellows out tequila's heat, for a punch that might just become your new summer go-to (or a Taco Tuesday mainstay year-round).

YIELD: 16 SERVINGS

---

3 cups tequila, chilled

2 cups fresh, strained grapefruit juice (from about 2 ruby red grapefruits)

1 cup fresh, strained lime juice (from about 8 to 10 limes)

1 cup Simple Syrup (page 164)

1 teaspoon kosher salt

1 bottle champagne, chilled

Combine chilled tequila, chilled grapefruit juice, lime juice, simple syrup, and salt in a punch bowl over 1 large block of ice. Stir rapidly until chilled, about 20 seconds, then top carefully with the chilled champagne. Ladle into small tumblers, with or without ice according to preference, and serve.

Note: *I like to garnish this punch with halved grapefruit slices and either rosemary sprigs in the fall and winter, or fennel blossoms (pictured) in the spring and summer. You can serve it in punch cups rather than tumblers, of course, but casual glassware feels most appropriate to the drink—when I bring it to parties, it often gets poured into plastic cocktail cups. Just make sure whatever vessel you serve it in isn't too large (no Ssolo cups allowed), since this punch is at full cocktail strength and you don't want your guests on the floor.*

GARDEN PARTY PUNCH

Tasting notes: bright fruit, citrus, floral, light, and refreshing

I created this punch as a vehicle for fresh, edible flowers, which are much easier to acquire in the spring and summer months, the perfect time of year for garden parties and other outdoor affairs. I use a variety, starting with highly aromatic blooms (rose and lavender are favorites) then layering in color and flavor—maybe bright, tart begonia or cucumber-like borage.

YIELD: 16 SERVINGS

---

3 cups gin, chilled

1 cup elderflower liqueur, chilled

1½ cups fresh, strained lemon juice (from about 6 to 8 lemons)

1½ cups fresh, strained grapefruit juice (from about 2 ruby red grapefruits)

1½ cups Simple Syrup (page 164)

1 teaspoon Peychaud's aromatic bitters

1 bottle champagne, chilled

About ½ to 1 cup flowers such as lavender, rose, viola, borage, begonia, calendula, dahlia, dianthus, hibiscus, nasturtium, or snapdragon, grown organically for culinary use

(1) Pour the chilled gin, chilled elderflower liqueur, lemon juice, grapefruit juice, simple syrup, and bitters into a punch bowl over 1 large block of ice. Stir rapidly until chilled, about 20 seconds.

(2) Top carefully with the chilled champagne, then garnish with a variety of edible flowers. Ladle a few flowers into each punch cup as you serve.

Note: *If you find edible flowers too cost-prohibitive or difficult to procure, sub in 1 teaspoon rosewater or orange blossom water, and garnish with halved grapefruit slices instead.*

Note: The best way to ensure that your edible flowers are clean, organic, and chemical-free for consumption is to grow them yourself (I use my edible flower garden for baking and teas just as much as I use it for garnishes). But you can still get food-safe blooms online before the growing season starts—even springtime is, after all, still fairly barren in many parts of the country. See page 166 for my source for year-round blooms.

RUSSIAN SPRING PUNCH

Tasting notes: tart, crisp, bright, berry

Created by renowned bartender Dick Bradsell in London as an inexpensive party drink, this punch (essentially a spiked Kir Royale) is quick to assemble and even quicker to please. Think of it as a sparkling black currant lemonade—tart and refreshing, with a vibrant berry hue.

YIELD: 16 SERVINGS

---

3 cups vodka, chilled

2 cups Simple Syrup (page 164), chilled

1½ cups fresh, strained lemon juice (from about 8 to 10 lemons), chilled

½ cup black currant liqueur (such as Clear Creek Distillery Cassis Liqueur), chilled

1 bottle champagne, chilled

Optional: blackberries or blackcurrants, for garnish

Pour the chilled vodka, chilled simple syrup, chilled lemon juice, and chilled liqueur into a punch bowl over 1 large block of ice. Stir rapidly until chilled, about 20 seconds, then top carefully with the chilled champagne. Ladle into chilled punch glasses or small, ice-filled tumblers.

*Note: As noted in the **Kir Royale** recipe (page 40), black currant liqueur's reputation has been slightly marred by the proliferation of overly sweetened, bottom-shelf "crème de cassis" liqueurs. Make sure you're using an authentic black currant product—I like Clear Creek Distillery's Cassis Liqueur, but Lejay is another good option.*

PERSIMMON PUNCH

Tasting notes: fall fruit and baking spice, warm vanilla, citrus

Persimmon season just happens to coincide almost exactly with the holidays in the US, from about October through February. Score some at your local market to make a seasonal punch that's as tasty as it is festive, particularly with backup players cinnamon and vanilla bean on hand.

YIELD: 6 TO 8 SERVINGS PER BATCH

---

1 cup gin

2 fuyu persimmons, thinly sliced

1 cinnamon stick

1 inch piece of vanilla bean, split (or ½ teaspoon vanilla extract)

4 tablespoons sugar

Chilled champagne, to top (about 1½ cups)

⅓ cup Aperol

⅓ cup fresh, strained grapefruit juice

¼ cup fresh, strained lemon juice

6 dashes Angostura aromatic bitters

(1) Infuse the gin (since this is the do-ahead part, make sure to multiply the recipe for as many batches as you plan to serve). Combine the gin, persimmon, cinnamon, and vanilla bean in a sealed container, then let sit at room temperature for 24 hours. Strain through a fine mesh sieve and store in the refrigerator. If using immediately, chill first in the freezer for 1 hour.

(2) In a small, freezer-chilled punch bowl, combine the sugar and a splash of the champagne. Muddle until the sugar is almost completely dissolved. Add ice (one large block or six king cubes), the infused gin, Aperol, grapefruit, lemon, and bitters, and stir until chilled (about 20 seconds). Top carefully with the chilled champagne, then ladle into chilled punch glasses and serve immediately.

Note: *This punch serves fewer people then most of the recipes in this chapter, but if you prep the ingredients beforehand, it comes together in less than a minute—just muddle, pour, and stir. This means you can easily replenish the bowl during your party.*

PICKING PERSIMMONS

There are quite a few varieties of persimmons out there, but for most cocktails (like the **Persimmon Punch**, page 78) it's best to stick to the fuyu persimmon, which is sweet and can be eaten while still a little firm. Fuyu persimmons are the ones that are squat, like a small heirloom tomato or donut peach. Hachiya persimmons (the ones shaped more like big, pointy acorns) will be sweet only when very, very ripe (think overripe). You can still use them, but wait until they're extremely soft before you cut into them, and then test a slice or two to make sure they don't taste astringent. You'll know an unripe, astringent persimmon when you taste it—the mouthfeel is notably odd, like cotton or fur.

SPICED PEAR PUNCH

Tasting notes: warm baking spice, smooth pear, bright citrus

Nothing finishes a holiday spread better than a gorgeous bowl of punch. Make the spiced pear syrup in advance, then assemble the rest quickly and easily the day of your party.

YIELD: 16 SERVINGS

---

3 cinnamon sticks (standard jar size, about 3 inches long each)

1 cup 100% pear juice, not from concentrate

1 cup sugar

2 cups Krogstad aquavit, chilled

2 cups amontillado sherry, chilled

1 cup fresh, strained lemon juice (from about 6 lemons)

1 bottle champagne, chilled

Optional: pear slices and rosemary sprigs, to garnish

(1) Break up the cinnamon sticks in the bottom of a sturdy saucepan until they are smallish shards (a wooden mallet or muddler works well for this). Add the pear juice and sugar. Bring to a boil, stirring occasionally, then lower heat and simmer, covered, for 5 minutes. Remove from heat and let stand, still covered, at room temperature overnight. Strain through a fine mesh sieve and use immediately or make ahead and store in the refrigerator (use within 1 week).

(2) Pour the aquavit, chilled sherry, cinnamon pear syrup, and lemon juice into a punch bowl filled with ice. Stir rapidly until chilled, about 10 seconds, then top carefully with the chilled champagne.

Note: This recipe can handle a fair amount of dilution, so you can use ice cubes rather than a large ice block. I prefer king cubes (they're more attractive than standard cubes and you need fewer of them) but have used bags of plain grocery store ice more than once in past, when travel or time didn't allow for the good stuff.

CHATHAM ARTILLERY PUNCH

Tasting notes: oak, vanilla, nutmeg, citrus, bright effervescence

Despite being one of the most famous champagne punches in American history, the actual recipe for Chatham Artillery Punch is more legend than law. The accounts of its makeup range widely, from a red wine, tea, and pineapple mixture, to a combination of gin, scotch, and maraschino cherries (still can't wrap my head around that one). I prefer the recipes that call for whiskey, brandy, and rum, tempered by sugar and citrus. In any case, imbibe carefully—this potent punch gained its historical notoriety by knocking famous military figures off their feet.

YIELD: 16 SERVINGS

1½ cups bourbon

1½ cups aged Jamaican rum (such as Appleton Estate Signature)

1½ cups Cognac (such as Pierre Ferrand Ambre)

2 cups Simple Syrup (page 164)

1 cup fresh, strained lemon juice (from about 6 lemons)

1 bottle champagne, chilled

Freshly grated nutmeg, to top

(1) Combine bourbon, rum, cognac, simple syrup, and lemon juice in a punch bowl, then cover and chill in the refrigerator for at least 2 hours and no longer than 8.

(2) Add a large block of ice, top carefully with the chilled champagne, then grate fresh nutmeg over top, just until fragrant and lightly covered all over. Serve with a ladle and punch glasses.

Note: *I absolutely love this punch with **Ginger Honey Syrup** (page 164) in place of the simple syrup, especially in the winter and fall.*

Note: *Whatever you do, don't skip the freshly grated nutmeg—it's not just a garnish, it's an integral part of the drink. You'll find jarred whole nutmeg in the spice section of most grocery stores, and a microplane works well for grating. If you prefer, you can grate it lightly over each punch glass rather than the whole bowl. A little bit goes a long way.*

SPICED GRAPEFRUIT PUNCH

Tasting notes: botanicals, cinnamon spice, bright, juicy citrus

Cinnamon and grapefruit are a match made in cocktail heaven—together, they just work. The complex and lightly bitter combination is reminiscent of tonic water, which is why it makes such a great foundation for gin. This is a punch that cries out to be noticed, and my guests always ask for the recipe.

YIELD: 16 SERVINGS

3 cups gin

1½ cups sweet vermouth (such as Carpano Antica)

2 cups Cinnamon Syrup (page 164)

3 cups fresh, strained grapefruit juice (from about 3 to 4 ruby red grapefruits)

1½ cups fresh, strained lemon juice (from about 10 to 12 lemons)

Optional: halved grapefruit slices, to garnish

1 bottle champagne, chilled

(1) Combine gin, sweet vermouth, syrup, grapefruit juice, and lemon juice in a punch bowl, then cover and chill in the refrigerator for at least 2 hours and no longer than 8.

(2) Add a large block of ice (and optional grapefruit slices), top carefully with the chilled champagne, and serve with a ladle and punch glasses.

*Note: Since the cinnamon syrup needs to be made ahead, I highly recommend making a double batch and using the leftovers to try some of the other cinnamon syrup cocktails in this book, like the **Spiced Tequila Tonic Sour** (page 144) or the **Spiced Scotch Pineapple Fizz** (page 138).*

THREE ACRE PUNCH

Tasting notes: smooth, citrusy, classic punch

I developed this recipe years ago, when I lived on a street called Three Acre Lane. I can still remember the first time I served it, because of the now legendary (in our household) shenanigans that transpired. Take warning: this is a potent punch. Smooth, crowd-pleasing, and eminently drinkable, it suits just about any occasion, but must be served responsibly. As the saying goes, it's an iron fist in a velvet glove.

YIELD: 16 SERVINGS

---

1 cup sugar

1 cup hot, freshly brewed black tea blend (see Note)

1½ cups aged Jamaican rum (such as Appleton Estate Signature)

1½ cups Cognac (such as Pierre Ferrand Ambre)

1½ cups Grand Marnier orange-flavored liqueur

½ cup fresh, strained lemon juice

½ cup fresh, strained lime juice

1 bottle champagne, chilled

(1) Add sugar to the hot tea, stirring frequently until completely dissolved. Let cool.

(2) Combine tea, rum, cognac, liqueur, lemon juice, and lime juice in a punch bowl, then cover and chill in the refrigerator for at least 2 hours and no longer than 8.

(3) Add a large block of ice, top carefully with the chilled champagne, and serve with a ladle and punch glasses.

Note: *I serve this punch throughout the year, so I choose my black tea blend according to season. For example, in the spring I frequently use Earl Grey, in the summer a peach blend, apple for fall, and cinnamon for winter.*

CHAPTER 4: BRUNCHES

MIMOSAS, BELLINIS, AND MORE

If this is a practical book of recipes for those life moments most likely to call for champagne, it only makes sense to devote an entire chapter to brunch. The **Bellini** and **Mimosa** are, of course, included, because although their list of ingredients may be small, making them correctly takes some thought.

If you're ready to step away from the usual subjects, you'll find some seasonal variations, and some recipes that don't involve fruit juice at all (if the mimosa/bellini family can be roughly defined as juice topped with champagne). I don't like to play favorites, but you should try the **Bubbly Mary** at least once if you're a fan of the original Bloody.

BELLINI

Tasting notes: fresh and juicy, bursting with the floral notes of ripe white peach

The simplest drinks can be the most important to make correctly—each detail is heightened by the lack of surrounding players to distract from mistakes or substitutions. A bad Bellini is a sad, thin shadow of its true self, wherein acrid, imitation "peach juice" stands undeserving of the prosecco it's mixed with. But a good Bellini deserves its legendary status as a brunch drink—intensely juicy, lightly floral, pale rose in color and perfectly refreshing.

YIELD: 1 COCKTAIL

---

1 ounce chilled white peach juice or puree (see sidebar, page 91)

Chilled champagne, to top (about 3 ounces)

Combine chilled peach juice or puree and chilled champagne in an empty, chilled mixing glass or metal shaking tin. Give a light stir, then pour into a chilled champagne glass.

THE PERFECT BELLINI

In Venice, the birthplace of the Bellini, many establishments will only serve you this drink while white peaches are actually in season, from May to September—a testament to the importance of using top-quality, ripe fruit in this recipe. Think of biting into an actual peach. When it's perfectly ripe, a peach is a true thing of beauty—summer in a bite, juices dripping down your chin. An unripe or overripe peach? Rock hard or mealy, barely edible. You know which one you want in your glass.

My favorite way to extract ripe peach juice for a Bellini is with a masticating juicer. If you don't have one of these, make a white peach puree by blending a few pitted white peaches with 1 teaspoon of lemon and 1 teaspoon vodka per peach (to prevent oxidation and browning while blending). Strain through a fine mesh sieve, then stir in simple syrup to taste—you want to achieve just the same level of sweetness as the original peach. Cover tightly and let chill before serving (about 3 hours in the coldest part of your refrigerator or one in your freezer). Use within 24 hours.

Why not pour the peach juice and prosecco directly into the glass? Peach juice (and especially peach puree) foams like crazy, which is why it's also very important to keep the ingredients and glasses for the cocktail ice-cold. Mixing the juice and prosecco in a separate vessel will cut down on some of the more unattractive, thick bubbles that rise up and dirty the sides of the glass for a cleaner look and taste. You'll still get about a quarter inch of lovely, fragrant foam on top—just not inches of big, sludgy bubbles. It also makes it easier to serve multiple Bellinis at a time—you can likely fit up to 4 in your mixing vessel, then pour them out into chilled champagne glasses all at once.

A traditional Bellini calls for 1 part peach juice to 3 parts prosecco, but some prefer the ratio of 2 parts peach juice to 3 parts prosecco. A simple way to decide is to start with the traditional version, then give the mixture a quick taste while it's still in the mixing vessel. Simply add more juice if you want more peach flavor before pouring the drink into the chilled champagne glass.

Finally, though it's decidedly not traditional, I personally love to add a half ounce of good-quality peach liqueur (such as G. E. Massenez or Giffard Crème de Pêche) to each cocktail for more backbone and complex peach flavor.

BUBBLY MARY

Tasting notes: tangy tomato, spicy horseradish, bright acidity, and peppery kick

If champagne cocktails like the Bellini and Mimosa are the reigning queens of brunch, then the Bloody Mary is surely king. Isn't it time we combined the two? Rich, sweet tomato juice can only benefit from the bright acidity of champagne. But a standard Bloody Mary mix is far too thick to play nicely with CO_2, with flecks of pepper and horseradish just waiting to burst into a sludgy foam. My version uses flavorful tomato (and horseradish) water instead, for a base just clarified enough to incorporate nicely into the bubbles, but not enough to lose the signature richness of the drink.

YIELD: 1 COCKTAIL

---

2 ounces Bubbly Mary Mix (page 94)

1 ounce chilled vodka

Chilled champagne to top (about 2 ounces)

Optional: salt, pepper, and celery salt, to rim

Combine the mix and the chilled vodka in a chilled champagne glass, then top carefully with chilled champagne.

Optional: prepare the glass in advance by wetting the edge with a cut lime, then dipping it in salt, pepper, and celery salt, to taste.

Note: Half the fun of a Bloody Mary can be in the garnish. Go as wild (or restrained) as you please but keep whatever's on your skewer (my favorite is cherry tomatoes) out of the liquid—you don't want it sitting in there causing excess fizz.

*Note: Swap chilled gin in place of the vodka for a **Bubbly Snapper** or blanco tequila for a **Bubbly Maria**.*

BUBBLY MARY MIX

YIELD: ABOUT 1½ CUPS, ENOUGH FOR 6 COCKTAILS

---

9 ounces tomato water, fresh or strained juice from a drained 28 ounce can of whole peeled tomatoes

½ ounce horseradish water (strained juice from a jar of prepared horseradish)

½ ounce Worcestershire

½ ounce hot sauce of choice

1½ ounces fresh, strained lime juice

¼ teaspoon salt

Combine tomato water, horseradish water, Worcestershire, hot sauce, lime juice, and salt in a container, stir until combined, cover and chill for at least 3 hours in the coldest part of the refrigerator or 1 hour in the freezer. If you make the mix more than 8 hours in advance, don't squeeze and strain the lime juice into the mix until just before serving.

Note: Substitute pickle juice for the hot sauce if you don't like heat.

MIMOSA

Tasting notes: crisp, juicy citrus with bright effervescence

Like its partner, the Bellini, a good Mimosa is all about nailing the details. Freshly squeezed OJ is a must, and a half ounce of orange liqueur gives the drink some necessary backbone. Put them together and top with champagne, and you've got a smooth, low Alcohol by Volume (ABV) cocktail brimming with orchard aromas and crisp acidity—a day drinker to end all others.

YIELD: 1 COCKTAIL

---

2 ounces fresh, strained orange juice

½ ounce Grand Marnier orange-flavored liqueur

Chilled champagne to top, (about 3 ounces)

Optional: 3 drops orange blossom water

Combine the orange juice and liqueur in a chilled champagne glass, then top carefully with chilled champagne.

Optional: top with 3 drops of orange blossom water.

Note: If you have the orange blossom water on hand (it's used more than once in this book), it adds some lovely, brunch-befitting floral top notes and completes the 1-2-3 punch (juice, liqueur, flower water) of orange flavor.

Note: For the best possible juice, squeeze and strain fresh oranges through a fine mesh sieve in advance, then chill in the coldest part of the refrigerator for 3 hours (or in the freezer for 1) to reduce foaming. The juice should be prepared as close to serving time as possible, and no more than 24 hours in advance.

ELDERFLOWER GRAPEFRUIT MIMOSA

Tasting notes: tart, floral, bittersweet, refreshing

Elderflower has a bright, almost lychee-like flavor that absolutely sings when paired with citrus. OJ gets all the usual brunch love, but grapefruit brings more acid and bitter complexity to the table. Try this once and see if it doesn't fast become your go-to mimosa for an easy brunch.

YIELD: 1 COCKTAIL

1½ ounces fresh, strained grapefruit juice, chilled

½ ounce chilled elderflower liqueur (such as St-Germain)

1 dash Angostura aromatic bitters

Chilled champagne to top, about 3 ounces

Combine the chilled grapefruit juice, chilled liqueur, and bitters in a chilled champagne glass. Top carefully with chilled champagne.

*Note: Grapefruit juice is more forgiving than lemon or lime—the flavors don't deteriorate as quickly, so you can juice them up to one day in advance (though you're always better off juicing as close to serving as possible). To make a batch of mix for a crowd (8 servings in total), do a **Grapefruit Mimosa Punch**: Combine 1½ cups fresh, strained grapefruit juice with ½ cup elderflower liqueur and 8 dashes Angostura in a sealed container, and chill in the coldest part of your refrigerator for at least 3 hours (or in the freezer for 1). When it's time to serve, divide evenly between 8 glasses (2 ounces of mix per glass) and top with the chilled champagne.*

PIMM'S ROYALE

Tasting notes: fruity, complex, lightly spiced, tart, refreshing

The Pimm's Cup is a quintessentially British summer cocktail, notably consumed by spectators at polo, cricket, and tennis matches in the United Kingdom. It's gaining in popularity stateside as well, and frankly, it's about time—this refreshing, lightly spiced, low-ABV cocktail seems tailor-made for day drinking. The addition of champagne lends a smooth, rounded acidity so seamless and welcome, it probably should have been there all along.

YIELD: 4 COCKTAILS

¾ cup Pimm's Cup No. 1 Liqueur

¼ cup gin (such as Plymouth)

Juice of 1 lemon, strained

4 strawberries, hulled

1 English cucumber, roughly chopped

2 tablespoons sugar

Chilled champagne, to top (about 3 ounces per drink)

Optional: additional fruit, to garnish

(1) In a blender, blend Pimm's, gin, lemon juice, strawberries, cucumber, and sugar on high speed just until the sugar has dissolved and the mixture is smooth. Strain through a fine mesh sieve and chill, covered, in the coldest part of the refrigerator for at least 3 hours (or in the freezer for 1). Make as close to serving time as possible, and no more than 12 hours in advance.

(2) Divide the mixture evenly between 4 chilled champagne glasses (about 2 ounces of mixture per glass), then top carefully with chilled champagne and fruit.

*Note: Like the **Bloody Mary**, you'll often see this drink garnished to the nines—usually with some combination of strawberries, cucumbers, apples, and citrus wheels. Go crazy, but keep your garnish skewered on the rim (out of the drink itself) to prevent foaming. My personal favorite? A big fennel flower—the blossoms taste like anise candy, a mouthwatering partner to the strawberries and spices in this drink. And fennel typically blooms midsummer, which just so happens to be prime Pimm's season.*

SPICY BLOOD ORANGE SERRANO MIMOSA

Tasting notes: spicy heat, lightly bitter, jammy citrus, agave

Citrus and spice are a match made in culinary heaven, especially when that citrus is the sweet, jammy, lightly floral blood orange. This one definitely packs some heat—serranos are generally spicier than jalapeños, so if you want to tone things down a bit, opt for that pepper instead (or infuse for half the recommended time). Tequila and Aperol lend bittersweet backbone for a cocktail as sturdy and complex as it is crisp and refreshing.

YIELD: 8 COCKTAILS

¾ cup blanco tequila

1 serrano chili pepper, thinly sliced

1 cup fresh, strained blood orange juice

¾ cup Aperol

8 dashes Peychaud's aromatic bitters

Chilled prosecco, to top (about 3 ounces per drink)

(1) Combine the tequila and serrano pepper in a sealed container and let sit at room temperature for 30 minutes, then strain out the pepper.

(2) Add the blood orange juice, Aperol, and bitters to the infused tequila, then cover and chill in the coldest part of the refrigerator for at least 3 hours (or in the freezer for 1). Mixture can be made up to 24 hours in advance.

(3) Divide the chilled mixture evenly between 8 chilled champagne glasses (about 2½ ounces per glass), then top carefully with the chilled prosecco.

Note: Like grapefruit juice, blood orange juice is more forgiving than lemon or lime—the flavors don't deteriorate as quickly, so you can juice the fruit up to one day in advance (though you're always better off juicing as close to serving as possible). You can also use regular oranges for this recipe if blood oranges are out of season—you'll lose the bold color and some of the jammier fruit notes, but these are barely perceptible to the average drinker.

APPLE CIDER MIMOSA

Tasting notes: juicy, bright, refreshing apple flavor

Pumpkin spice gets all the love when the leaves start to turn, but to me there's no better indication that fall is truly here than to see fresh, local apple cider (unfiltered apple juice) start to hit the shelves. It's become so popular in recent years that I can usually find it year-round (get it from the refrigerated section, not the aisles), though the best time to drink and serve it is naturally in season. If you're lucky enough to live in an area with apple orchards, you may even be lucky enough to snag some cold pasteurized, or even unpasteurized, juice—the best kind.

YIELD: 1 COCKTAIL

---

1 ounce chilled apple cider (unfiltered apple juice)

½ ounce chilled Grand Marnier orange-flavored liqueur

¼ ounce fresh, strained lime juice

Chilled champagne, to top (about 3 ounces)

Optional: sliced apple, to garnish

Combine the chilled apple cider, chilled liqueur, and lime juice in a chilled champagne flute. Top carefully with chilled champagne.

Optional: create a sliced apple fan to garnish by skewering 3-5 very thin apple slices in a stack, then pulling the ends apart like a fan.

*Note: Apples are versatile flavor partners and can go pair with a slew of liqueurs besides the orange used here. For an **Elderflower Apple Cider Mimosa**, swap St-Germain for the Grand Marnier. For a **Maraschino Apple Cider Mimosa**, swap Luxardo for the Grand Marnier.*

ROSEMARY MAPLE BELLINI

Tasting notes: juicy peach, woody rosemary, rich maple, crisp effervescence

Real maple syrup is a cocktail hero of mine. I always have some in the refrigerator (it keeps almost indefinitely—about a year), just waiting to be called into service when I don't have the energy to make a syrup or want to add a rich caramel complexity to any drink. Paired here with juicy peach and woody rosemary, it's an autumnal masterpiece— particularly in early fall, when peaches are still in season.

YIELD: 1 COCKTAIL

1 sprig rosemary

1 ounce chilled peach juice or puree

¼ ounce fresh, strained lemon juice

¼ ounce real maple syrup

Chilled prosecco, to top (about 3 ounces)

Optional: peach slices and edible leaves (such as hibiscus) or decorative leaves (such as maple), to garnish

(1) Rub the sprig of rosemary around the inside and edges of a chilled champagne glass.

(2) Pour the chilled peach juice, lemon juice, and maple syrup into the prepared glass, then stir gently until the syrup dissolves completely. Top carefully with the chilled prosecco.

Optional: create a sliced peach fan to garnish by skewering 3 very thin peach slices in a stack, then pulling the ends apart like a fan. Balance on a skewer placed across the rim with a leaf (maple pictured) or additional rosemary.

*Note: You can use peach nectar in a pinch. The flavors are more cooked and jam-like, but the rich caramel notes of the syrup make them work as they wouldn't in a classic **Bellini**, which relies more heavily on fresh floral flavor. See **The Perfect Bellini** (page 91).*

MEYER LEMON LAVENDER BELLINI

Tasting notes: complex florals, bright acidity, juicy peach

To compliment the abundance of easy brunch options in this chapter, this one requires a little more elbow grease—but with a vibrantly, almost indescribably complex floral payoff. Starting with the delicate floral sweetness of a ripe white peach, we layer in the bergamot fragrance of a Meyer lemon peel, then cap it all off with woodsy lavender. The good news is that although the base mixture requires some effort, you can make it in advance, so that when brunch rolls around all you have to do is pour.

I make this mixture via the sous vide method, but don't worry if you don't have the gear—anyone can achieve similar results by letting the mixture of peels, fruit, flowers, juice, and sugar sit overnight before straining.

YIELD: ABOUT 10 COCKTAILS

---

6 to 8 lemons (enough for 1 cup juice)

1 cup sugar

2 white peaches, roughly chopped, skin on

2 teaspoons lavender buds

Chilled prosecco, to top (about 3 ounces per cocktail)

(1) Using a peeler, remove the zest from the citrus in wide strips, avoiding the bitter white pith as much as possible. Use a paring knife to slice or scrape off any excess pith from each strip. Juice and strain the zested lemons until you have 1 cup juice, then add it to a blender along with the sugar. Blend on high speed until the sugar dissolves.

(2) **If using the sous vide method**, carefully transfer the peels and juice/sugar mixture to a plastic bag, then add the chopped peaches and

continued . . .

continued from page 106

lavender and seal according to sous vide instructions. Submerge in a 135°F water bath for 2 hours, then plunge bag into an ice bath to cool. Strain and use immediately, or store in the fridge for up to 2 weeks. ***If using the overnight method***, combine the peels and juice/sugar mixture with the peaches and lavender in a tightly sealed container, then let sit in the fridge overnight (or at least 8 hours). Strain and use immediately, or store in the fridge for up to 2 weeks.

(3) For the cocktail, pour 1½ ounce of the mixture into a chilled champagne glass and top carefully with chilled prosecco.

Note: *If you don't make 10 of these at a time and have leftover Meyer lemon/peach/ lavender cordial, drizzle it over ice cream or pound cake, or add it to plain seltzer for a heck of a soda.*

Note: *White peaches, in season from May to September, are best for Bellinis, but yellow peaches make a fine substitute when white can't be found. Since you'll be infusing these peaches with their skin on (the fragrant skin is a crucial element here), try to use organic if possible.*

MELON MINT MIMOSA

Tasting notes: cool mint, refreshing, juicy melon

Fresh, ripe honeydew is a fantastic partner to prosecco, whose flavor profile often includes melon within its predominantly fruit and flower notes. The addition of mint makes this recipe especially cool and refreshing—I can't imagine a better summer brunch cocktail, which begs to be sipped in the hot sunshine.

YIELD: ABOUT 6 COCKTAILS

½ **ripe honeydew melon**

2 ounces vodka

2 ounces sugar

1 ounce fresh, strained lemon juice

2 heaping palmfuls fresh mint leaves

Chilled prosecco, to top (about 3 ounces per drink)

(1) Scoop out the flesh of the honeydew, discarding the seeds, and add to a blender, along with the vodka, sugar, lemon juice, and mint. Blend on high speed just until smooth, only about 5 seconds.

(2) Strain the mixture through a fine mesh sieve, then cover and chill in the freezer until very cold, about 1 hour.

(3) Pour 2 ounces of the mixture into each chilled champagne glass, then top carefully with chilled prosecco.

Note: *Mint is notoriously delicate and volatile—the best aromas dissipate quickly, so prepare the base mixture as close to serving as you can.*

STRAWBERRY THAI BASIL FIZZ

Tasting notes: fresh strawberry, anise spice, herbaceous, bright

Strawberries and Thai basil, known for its spicy anise aroma, make one of my favorite sweet and savory combinations—just try them in a salad together and see if I'm not wrong. An overnight infusion requires little prep (simply slice the strawberries and submerge them in a liqueur), with loads of fresh flavor and easy day-of assembly.

YIELD: ABOUT 8 COCKTAILS

---

6 strawberries, thinly sliced

20 medium-to-large Thai basil leaves

1 cup Grand Marnier orange-flavored liqueur

Chilled sparkling rosé, to top (about 3 ounces per drink)

Optional: strawberry slice, to garnish

(1) Combine the strawberries, basil, and liqueur in sealed container and let sit at room temperature for 8 hours or overnight. Strain through a fine mesh sieve and let chill in the refrigerator, covered, for at least 3 hours (or 1 hour in the freezer).

(2) For each cocktail, pour 1 ounce of the infusion into a chilled champagne glass, then top carefully with chilled sparkling rosé.

Optional: cut a slit in the strawberry slice and perch it on the rim of the glass.

Note: The strained, covered infusion will keep in the refrigerator for up to 3 days, but it is best prepared as close to serving as possible.

SOLE ROSSO

Tasting notes: bright citrus, tart, bittersweet, refreshing

A seasonal take on the Aperol Spritz, with the decidedly brunch-appropriate addition of blood orange juice and its signature deep red hue. Low in alcohol and high on simplicity—no shaking, stirring, or syrups included—it's the very definition of easygoing.

YIELD: 1 COCKTAIL

---

2 ounces chilled Aperol

¾ ounce fresh, strained blood orange juice

Chilled prosecco, to top (about 2 ounces)

Halved blood orange slice and rosemary, to garnish

Pour the chilled Aperol and blood orange juice into an ice-filled glass (rocks or wine glasses both work well), then top carefully with the chilled prosecco. Garnish with a halved orange slice and a sprig of rosemary.

__Note:__ Since this recipe is incredibly quick to make, I like to use my extra prep time to brûlée the orange slices for garnish: Simply dip one side in sugar and heat with a kitchen torch until lightly charred.

CHAPTER 5:
DECEPTIVELY SIMPLE

FLAVOR WITHOUT FUSS

Though each of these cocktails is as complex and flavorful as any other in the book, they all have at least one element that makes them easier than most to assemble.

Many of them require no shaking or stirring. None require infusions. Only a few require syrups, and the syrups required can be made in minutes. This is a chapter of no-nonsense cocktails for the inevitable moments when you don't have much time or energy to spare, but still want something interesting to sip on or serve.

Champagne has a reputation for grandeur and refinement, but it's actually a particularly handy ingredient for the quick-and-easy category. Most great cocktails rely on some combination of sugar and acid to work their flavor magic—even a Martini has acid in the form of vermouth. Since champagne is acidic (it has both tartaric and lactic acid, plus the sharp, prickly flavor of carbonation), including it in a cocktail means you're already well on your way to an ideal sugar:acid balance. In other words, you don't need to add much to it to achieve great flavor.

ORANGE BLOSSOM

Tasting notes: light, crisp, floral, citrusy

This is one of those cocktails so simple in execution but complex in flavor it belongs on everyone's short list. Have it up your sleeve for those nights when big impact but small effort is called for—last-minute guests, holiday parties, or even a low-key weeknight. When you can't manage much, you can still manage this cocktail. Bright, bold citrus and elegant floral notes suit every occasion.

YIELD: 1 COCKTAIL

---

1 ounce Grand Marnier orange-flavored liqueur, chilled

3 drops orange blossom water

Chilled champagne to top (about 4 ounces)

Optional: decorative or edible flower, to garnish

Pour the chilled Grand Marnier and orange blossom water into a chilled champagne glass. Top with chilled champagne.

Optional: garnish with edible flower.

__Note:__ Orange blossom water may take a bit of tracking down, but it makes a great permanent pantry item. It lends a wonderful floral top note to anything you put it in (cocktails, of course, but also sweets) with a slightly bitter finish. Try a few drops in your next gin drink or creamy dessert, like panna cotta or crème brulée, and prepare to be amazed. Look for it in the international section of your grocery store or order it online. And don't try to pour a few drops directly from the bottle— you're sure to overdo it. Drugstores sell medicine droppers very cheaply that will make this step both easy and accurate.

WATERMELON COCONUT COOLER

Tasting notes: juicy, fruit forward, refreshing

I originally created this cocktail for a pool party, when my friends requested something light and juicy with no refined sugar. Fresh watermelon and coconut water make the drink particularly hydrating, while a low-alcohol content makes it appropriate for daytime drinking in the hot sun. Though watermelon juice will take a few extra minutes to prepare in advance, the rest of the drink is simply layered in the glass—no shaking or stirring required.

YIELD: 1 COCKTAIL

---

1 ounce vodka

1 ounce coconut water, not from concentrate (such as Harmless Harvest)

1 ounce fresh watermelon juice (page 122)

Chilled prosecco to top (about 2 ounces)

Optional: lime wedge, coarse salt, and fresh herb leaves, to garnish

(1) Chill vodka, coconut water, watermelon juice, and prosecco in advance in the coldest part of your refrigerator for at least 3 hours.

(2) Optional: partially rim the glass by dragging a lime wedge over half of the edge and dipping it in a small plate or bowl filled with coarse salt. Garnish with a fresh herb of choice, such as fennel fronds, mint, or celery leaves.

(3) In a chilled rocks glass, pour the chilled vodka, coconut water, and 1 ounce watermelon juice over one king watermelon cube. Top carefully with the prosecco.

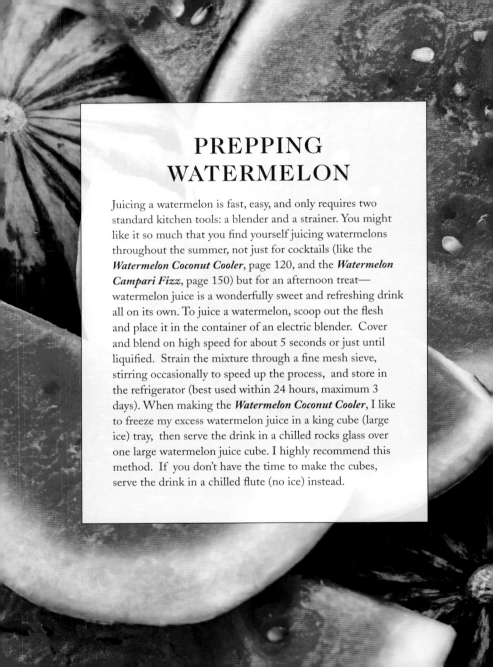

PREPPING WATERMELON

Juicing a watermelon is fast, easy, and only requires two standard kitchen tools: a blender and a strainer. You might like it so much that you find yourself juicing watermelons throughout the summer, not just for cocktails (like the *Watermelon Coconut Cooler*, page 120, and the *Watermelon Campari Fizz*, page 150) but for an afternoon treat—watermelon juice is a wonderfully sweet and refreshing drink all on its own. To juice a watermelon, scoop out the flesh and place it in the container of an electric blender. Cover and blend on high speed for about 5 seconds or just until liquified. Strain the mixture through a fine mesh sieve, stirring occasionally to speed up the process, and store in the refrigerator (best used within 24 hours, maximum 3 days). When making the *Watermelon Coconut Cooler*, I like to freeze my excess watermelon juice in a king cube (large ice) tray, then serve the drink in a chilled rocks glass over one large watermelon juice cube. I highly recommend this method. If you don't have the time to make the cubes, serve the drink in a chilled flute (no ice) instead.

GROVE APPEAL

Tasting notes: bright, tropical fruit, citrus, light baking spice

Bursting with fresh citrus and fruit-forward Jamaican rum, this cocktail tastes like it came straight from an orange grove somewhere in the Caribbean—and yet it requires no straining or squeezing, thanks to the inclusion of orange liqueur. If you want a lightly tropical drink but don't have fresh citrus on hand, this cocktail has your back.

YIELD: 1 COCKTAIL

¾ ounce aged Jamaican rum (such as Appleton Estate Signature)

¾ ounce Grand Marnier orange-flavored liqueur

1 dash Angostura bitters

Chilled champagne (about 2 ounces), to top

(1) Fill a chilled mixing glass or metal shaking tin with ice, then pour the rum, liqueur, and bitters into the vessel. Stir rapidly with a metal bar spoon for 15 seconds, then strain into a chilled champagne glass.

(2) Top with chilled champagne, by pouring carefully and slowly down the side of the glass to reduce foam.

Note: *Try it with tequila for a sharper, "hotter" (boozy on the palate) take—just make sure it's the añejo, or aged, variety. The lightly oaked caramel and vanilla notes pair particularly well with orange.*

HIBISCUS FIZZ

Tasting notes: refreshing, tart, lightly sweet, and floral

This low-ABV cocktail is a favorite of mine for daytime occasions, particularly in the warmer months—I've served it on porches, beaches, and backyards. Vibrant in color and tart in flavor, hibiscus tastes more like a cranberry than a flower. In a chapter focused on simplicity, this is the only recipe to use a homemade syrup—in this case, it's so easy to make it doesn't feel particularly burdensome. Simply brew your hibiscus tea as usual, add sugar and stir.

YIELD: 1 COCKTAIL

¾ **ounce Hibiscus Syrup (page 165)**

½ **ounce fresh, strained lemon juice**

Chilled champagne to top (about 5 ounces)

Optional: lemon wheel or a few drops of rosewater, to garnish

Pour the syrup and lemon juice into a chilled champagne glass, then top carefully with chilled champagne.

Optional: garnish with an edible flower (such as hibiscus or lavender) or a few drops of rosewater.

Note: To dress up this cocktail, dip the lemon wheel in crushed, dried flower petals. Dried rosebuds (pictured) are readily available online and in specialty tea stores, and can be crushed between your forefinger and thumb—no need to involve a muddler.

Note: The natural tartness of hibiscus coupled with lemon gives this recipe a strong but pleasant pucker. If you're not the biggest fan of the "sour" family, try cutting the lemon juice back to ¼ ounce for a smoother, sweeter version.

*Note: Turn this basic recipe into a **Hibiscus 75** by adding 1½ ounces of gin, ¾ ounce hibiscus syrup, and ½ ounce lemon juice to a shaker filled with ice, shaking for 15 seconds, straining into a chilled glass, and topping with champagne (only about 2 ounces in this case).*

MARGARITA FIZZ

Tasting notes: sharp, fresh, crisp, tart, citrus

Margarita fans (aren't we all?): this might just be a game changer for you. All of the tart, juicy lime and sharp tequila spice of the original, enlivened by a little joyful effervescence. Bubbles bring some of tequila's more subtle notes right to the nose—you'll be surprised at the pure agave or bright grassy aromas you'll be able to distinguish in this version. If there's a better stiff drink for a hot day out there, I've yet to find it.

YIELD: 1 COCKTAIL

Optional: lime wedge
and salt, to rim

1½ ounces blanco tequila

¾ ounce Grand Marnier
orange-flavored liqueur

½ ounce fresh, strained
lime juice

¼ ounce Simple Syrup
(page 164)

Pinch of salt

Chilled champagne, to top

Optional: to rim the glass, wet the rim of a chilled champagne glass with a cut lime, then dip it lightly in coarse salt to coat. Set aside.

(1) Combine the tequila, liqueur, lime juice, syrup, and salt in a cocktail shaker filled with ice. Shake hard for 15 seconds, then strain into the prepared salted glass or a plain chilled champagne glass.

(2) Top with chilled champagne, by pouring carefully and slowly down the side of the glass to reduce foam.

Note: *For a spicy version, try a **Jalapeño Margarita Fizz:** Infuse the tequila beforehand. Combine 1 cup of blanco tequila with 1 thinly sliced jalapeño pepper, let stand at room temperature for 30 minutes, then strain through a fine mesh sieve and store in the fridge.*

SORBET FLOAT

Tasting notes: sweet, tart, rich with frozen fruit

Here's the thing: this recipe is almost too simple to be called a recipe, but it's so frequently invoked in my household as an easy, impressive dessert, it needs to be mentioned here. Equally at home during the summer and winter holidays (I've served it both at an upscale New Year's affair and a casual backyard 4th of July barbecue), this dish defies seasonality. Champagne and fruit are just meant to be together, and a frozen puree in the form of a sorbet is the easiest way to access fresh fruit year-round.

YIELD: 1 COCKTAIL

---

1 scoop sorbet of choice

Optional: 3 drops orange blossom water and 1 black berry or other fresh fruit, to garnish

Chilled champagne to top (about 3 ounces)

Place the scoop of sorbet in a chilled dessert bowl and add 3 drops of orange blossom water (optional). Top with the chilled champagne, pouring directly over the scoop. Garnish with fresh fruit.

__Note:__ Since this recipe so incredibly simple, it will only be as delicious as the sorbet you serve it with. I like to get mine from a local homemade ice cream shop rather than the grocery store, for stand out flavors and ingredients like fresh berries and cardamom (Bent Spoon, New Jersey), rosemary (Oddfellows, New York), edible flowers (Salt & Straw, Oregon), frosé (Jeni's, Ohio), or rosewater (Owowcow, Pennsylvania). And you can always make your own if don't have options nearby.

IN CONCLUSION

Tasting notes: sharp, herbaceous, botanical, crisp

This recipe is a sparkling version of the vintage Last Word cocktail. It's every bit as sharp, tart, and herbaceous as the original, but with more refreshing acidity and peppy effervescence. The addition of sparkling wine opens up each flavor and gives it room to breathe, which is why I consider it to be more like a concluding paragraph than a final word.

YIELD: 1 COCKTAIL

½ **ounce gin**

½ **ounce green Chartreuse**

½ **ounce maraschino liqueur (such as Luxardo)**

½ **ounce fresh, strained lime juice**

Chilled champagne, to top

Optional: herb sprig or maraschino cherry, to garnish

(1) Combine the gin, Chartreuse, liqueur, and lime juice in a cocktail shaker filled with ice. Shake hard for 15 seconds, then strain into a chilled champagne glass.

(2) Top with chilled champagne, by pouring carefully and slowly down the side of the glass to reduce foam.

Optional: garnish with an herb sprig (such as rosemary) or a skewered maraschino cherry.

__Note:__ If you garnish with an herb sprig, flatter herbs like the kinome leaf pictured here can be affixed to the side of the glass with edible glue and a small paintbrush, available at most craft stores (I use edible glue because it washes off easily and doesn't damage my glassware). Woodier herbs like rosemary can be balanced on the rim of the glass—don't drop it in, or you'll lose effervescence too quickly. If you garnish with the cherry, make sure it's a real maraschino cherry, like Luxardo— don't put a Shirley Temple cherry on such a grown-up drink.

BITTER SHERRY FIZZ

Tasting notes: bitter spice, caramel oak, bright citrus, dried fruit

The rich texture, intensely nutty aroma, and tangy acidity of a good amontillado sherry make it a natural partner for the complex baking spice and bitter root characteristic of Angostura bitters—and it can handle a whole lot of them. If you're already a fan of all things bitter and never met an amaro you didn't like, this one is definitely for you.

YIELD: 1 COCKTAIL

2 ounces chilled amontillado sherry

½ ounce Simple Syrup (page 164)

¼ ounce fresh, strained lemon juice

¼ ounce Angostura aromatic bitters

Chilled champagne, to top (about 2 ounces)

Orange wedge and (optional) maraschino cherry (such as Luxardo) to garnish

Pour the sherry, syrup, lemon juice, and bitters into a rocks glass filled with ice. Stir lightly, then top carefully with chilled champagne. Garnish with an orange wedge and (optional) maraschino cherry.

Note: *Angostura bitters, so ubiquitous as a dash here and there, doesn't get enough attention as an ingredient in its own right. If you like this bitter fizz, give the* **Seelbach** *(page 35) a try.*

BLACK VELVET

Tasting notes: bitter, fruity, toasty, crisp, refreshing

This cocktail could have appeared in the classics chapter, since it's been around quite some time—it was allegedly created to mourn the passing of Queen Victoria's husband Albert, when a bartender felt that even champagne should be wearing black. If you're a fan of Irish stouts, generally known to be rich and creamy, you'll be amazed at the subtle fruit flavors unearthed by the addition of sparkling wine. Another upside to this drink? It stretches out your champagne—one bottle will go twice as far.

YIELD: 1 COCKTAIL

Chilled champagne (about 4 ounces)

Chilled Irish stout (such as Guinness Draught, about 4 ounces)

Fill a chilled highball glass halfway with chilled champagne, then fill to the top with chilled Irish stout.

Note: This cocktail is often poured in two distinct layers, with the Guinness "floated" (poured carefully over the back of a bar spoon so as not to mix the two) over the champagne. I prefer the flavor and experience of this drink fully mixed, so I don't employ this method—the density of the beer will make it self-incorporate into the champagne when poured without a spoon. But the layered look is an undeniably attractive visual, so if you want to put on a bit of a show, you can give the float method a try.

Note: You can use any chilled glassware here, but I prefer a chilled highball glass because the shape—a pure cylinder—makes it easier to visually gauge capacity with accuracy. In other words, it's best for seeing when exactly you've filled halfway. Additionally, the size of most highball glasses (8 to 10 ounces) is ideal for this drink.

CHAPTER 6:
WORTH THE EFFORT

TAKE IT TO THE NEXT LEVEL

In essence, none of these recipes are particularly difficult—they require no extra set of skills, no particular kitchen or cocktail knowledge. Most of them just require a little more time, an infusion, or homemade syrup. But I promise that no infusion or syrup in this book requires more than a few minutes of active prep time, or 24 hours of sitting on a counter to infuse.

If you can chop, simmer, and strain, you can make any of the cocktails in this chapter. In all honesty, they take less effort than making soup. And every single one of them is worth the effort—they're some of my favorite cocktails in this book.

The **Scandi 75** (page 136) has become my go-to drink for winter entertaining, and presents no harder hurdles than tracking down aquavit (look for it near the gin, ask your local liquor store to order it special, or find it online—one bottle will likely last all winter) and mixing up some honey syrup (simply stir hot tap water into honey—a 30-second process). With your leftover honey syrup, you can easily make the **Honeysuckle Fizz** (page 152), a bright and bubbly version of the classic Daiquiri, with no extra labor. In short, mixing your way through this chapter will be more manageable than you think, rewarding you with drinks that look and taste far more impressive than the effort it took to make them.

SCANDI 75

Tasting notes: star anise, bright, citrusy, refreshing

A wintry take on the classic French 75, this recipe showcases the Scandinavian spirit aquavit: a neutral spirit distilled from grain or potato and then flavored with a wide range of spices and botanicals. It's become a mainstay at my holiday table, and the drink I crave most when the temperature starts to drop.

YIELD: 1 COCKTAIL

Optional: pineapple wedge, to garnish

1½ ounces Krogstad aquavit

½ ounce fresh, strained lime juice

½ ounce Honey Syrup (page 164)

Chilled champagne, to top (about 2 ounces)

Optional: 1 star anise pod, to garnish

Optional, to garnish: before you mix the cocktail, char a pineapple wedge on a grill or under a broiler set to medium high, just until lightly blackened. Use a cocktail pick to balance the charred wedge on the rim of a chilled glass.

(1) Combine the aquavit, lime juice, and honey syrup in a cocktail shaker filled with ice. Shake hard for 15 seconds, then strain into a chilled champagne glass.

(2) Top with chilled champagne, by pouring carefully and slowly down the side of the glass to reduce foam.

Optional: garnish with a star anise pod.

Note: *Aquavit is a lot like gin—it comes in a wide variety of dominant flavors, from caraway or anise to dill, fennel, coriander, and citrus. I use Krogstad in this recipe for its heavy anise flavor, then garnish with a single star anise pod. Float the star anise pod in the drink itself, or perch it on a glass by removing one segment and balancing it on the gap.*

SPICED SCOTCH PINEAPPLE FIZZ

Tasting notes: campfire, cinnamon, tropical fruit, bright citrus

This cocktail is a cold-season drink hiding in tiki's wardrobe—smoky peat notes from the scotch and a kick of cinnamon spice say "autumn," while the pineapple and lime take a distinctly tropical bent. Essentially a spiced, sparkling whiskey sour, but a lot more fun.

YIELD: 1 COCKTAIL

1 ounce blended scotch

½ ounce Cinnamon Syrup (page 164)

½ ounce pineapple juice

¼ ounce fresh, strained lime juice

1 dash Angostura aromatic bitters

Chilled champagne (about 1 ounce), to top

(1) Combine the scotch, cinnamon syrup, pineapple juice, lime juice, and bitters in a cocktail shaker filled with ice. Shake hard for 15 seconds, then strain into a chilled champagne glass.

(2) Top carefully with the chilled champagne.

Note: *If you have a single malt scotch like Laphroaig in your collection and want to amp up the peaty smoke aroma, rise the glass with a splash beforehand.*

HOLIDAY MAIL

Tasting notes: bright, spicy ginger, tropical fruit, citrus

A touch of fresh ginger lends welcome spice to the vintage Airmail cocktail. The name brings to mind all of the holiday cards flying across the world as winter approaches. Though the flavors here are decidedly sunny and Caribbean, aged rum is always at home in the cold weather months.

YIELD: 1 COCKTAIL

1½ ounces aged Jamaican rum (such as Appleton Estate Signature)

½ ounce fresh, strained lime juice

¾ ounce Ginger Honey Syrup (page 165)

Chilled champagne, to top (about 1 ounce)

Optional: candied ginger, to garnish

(1) Combine the rum, lime juice, and ginger honey syrup in a cocktail shaker filled with ice. Shake hard for 15 seconds, then strain into a chilled champagne glass.

(2) Top with chilled champagne, by pouring carefully and slowly down the side of the glass to reduce foam.

Optional: garnish with candied ginger.

Note: *You can experiment with any aged rum you may have on hand, just be wary of the varying levels of sweetness—an older, smoother, sweeter rum may require more citrus for balance.*

CITRUS CORDIAL

Tasting notes: crisp, refreshing, and lightly sweet with bright, bold citrus

Meyer lemons, pomelos, blood oranges—my favorite way to show off the nuances in each variety of citrus is by making each into a pure citrus cordial (i.e., a juice and peel syrup) sous vide, then topping them off with champagne. Adding the peels unlocks all of the citrus's most complex floral and bitter notes, which you just can't access by using the juice alone. Don't worry if you don't have the gear—anyone can achieve similar results by letting the mixture of peels, juice, and sugar sit overnight before straining.

YIELD: 1 COCKTAIL, PLUS EXTRA CITRUS CORDIAL

Fresh, organic citrus (for every cup of cordial, you will need about ¾ cup citrus juice)

Sugar

Chilled champagne, to top (about 4 ounces)

Citrus twist, to garnish

(1) Using a peeler, remove the zest from the citrus in wide strips, avoiding the bitter white pith as much as possible. Use a paring knife to slice or scrape off any excess pith from each strip.

(2) Juice the citrus, then weigh the juice on a kitchen scale (alternate method: measure by volume in a measuring cup). Add the juice to a blender, then weigh or measure out an equal amount of sugar and add that to the blender as well. Blend on high speed until the sugar dissolves.

(3) **If using the sous vide method**, carefully transfer the peels and juice/sugar mixture to a plastic bag, then seal according to sous vide instructions. Submerge in a 135°F water

continued . . .

continued from page 141

bath for 2 hours, then plunge bag into an ice bath to cool. Strain and use immediately, or store in the fridge for up to 2 weeks.

If using the overnight method, combine the peels and juice/sugar mixture in a tightly sealed container, and let sit in the fridge overnight (or at least 8 hours). Strain and use immediately, or store in the fridge for up to two weeks.

(4) Add ¾ ounce of citrus cordial to a chilled champagne glass, then top carefully with chilled champagne. Garnish with fresh citrus twist.

Note: *You can make any citrus into a citrus cordial using this recipe. Each one will have a slightly different acid level, and a completely different bouquet of aromas and bright citrus flavors. They're all so good you'll want to drizzle them over your morning yogurt, or your evening ice cream (both of which I highly recommend).*

Note: *It's important to go organic here, because you're cooking with the peel, which growers don't have to consider edible and are likely to spray with all sorts of bad-tasting stuff, which will absolutely affect the way your syrup tastes.*

Citrus Cordial (pages 141–142)

SPICED TEQUILA TONIC SOUR

Tasting notes: bright, bitter, refreshing, baking spice

This strange little sipper is like a New York Sour, a margarita, and a quinquina got together and had a delicious, cinnamon-spiced baby over crushed ice—in other words, it more or less defies categorization. These ingredients may seem like odd bedfellows. But, taken together, the aromatics on display sing like a chorus.

YIELD: 1 COCKTAIL

1½ ounces tequila

½ ounce fresh, strained lime juice

½ ounce Cinnamon Syrup (page 164)

2 ounces chilled tonic water

Chilled Lambrusco secco (dry), to top (1 ounce)

Optional: lime wheel and blackberry, to garnish

(1) Fill a chilled rocks glass with crushed ice, then top with the tequila, lime juice, and cinnamon syrup. Stir lightly just until combined.

(2) Top first with the chilled tonic water, then with the chilled lambrusco. Serve with a straw.

Optional: garnish with a lime wheel and blackberry.

Note: To layer the Lambrusco attractively over the drink, pour carefully over the back of a bar spoon.

Note: Since the drink is being poured over crushed ice and thus losing most of its carbonation, you can go ahead and measure the tonic water instead of free pouring—the carbonation lost by transfer contact won't be noticeable at these levels.

RHUBARB 75

Tasting notes: tart, refreshing, floral, with warm vanilla

Tangy, tart, candy-colored rhubarb adds a vibrant seasonal touch to the classic French 75. The seasonal syrup used to make this drink is one of my all-time favorites, and it can be used in place of simple syrup in just about any cocktail for a cheerful dose of bright, fragrant spring flavor.

YIELD: 1 COCKTAIL

1½ ounces gin (such as Plymouth)

¾ ounce fresh, strained lemon juice

¾ ounce Rhubarb Syrup (page 164)

Chilled champagne, to top (about 2 ounces)

Optional: rhubarb ribbons, to garnish

(1) Combine the gin, lemon juice, and rhubarb syrup in a cocktail shaker filled with ice. Shake hard for 15 seconds, then strain into a chilled champagne glass.

(2) Top with chilled champagne, by pouring carefully and slowly down the side of the glass to reduce foam.

Optional: garnish with rhubarb ribbons.

Note: *I use a mandolin or a very sharp peeler to cut down rhubarb stalks into ribbons, then arrange them on the inside of chilled flutes with the help of a chopstick prior to pouring. Rhubarb that's a few days old tends to work better than freshly cut rhubarb for this because of its flexibility. If you can't manage picture-perfect ribbons (they are admittedly hard to arrange just so), let the curls dangle over the edge of the glass or simply float them on top. The added aroma is more important than the visual.*

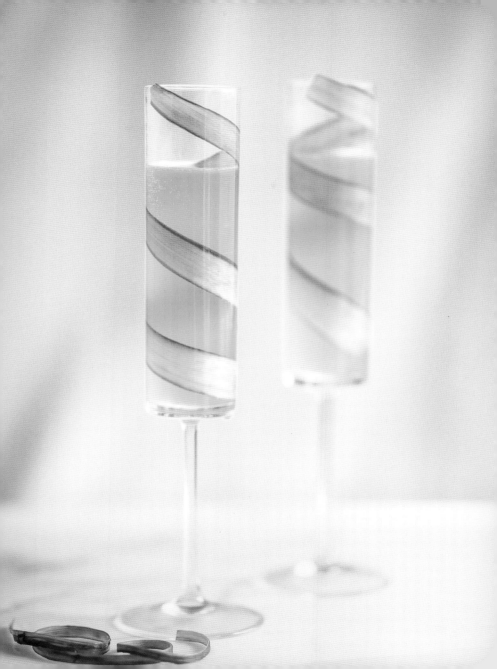

HONEY GINGER CHAMPAGNE MULE

Tasting notes: highly refreshing with spicy ginger, bright lime, light honey sweetness

Like a Moscow Mule, but much, much better. Champagne is a major upgrade on standard soda when paired with a homemade, lightly spicy ginger honey syrup. Dangerously smooth and impossibly refreshing, it's a true party starter and crowd-pleaser.

YIELD: 1 COCKTAIL

---

1 ounce vodka

¾ ounce Ginger Honey Syrup (page 165)

½ ounce fresh, strained lime juice

Chilled champagne, to top (about 3 ounces)

Optional: candied ginger or honeycomb, to garnish

(1) Combine the vodka, ginger honey syrup, and lime juice in a cocktail shaker filled with ice. Shake hard for 15 seconds, then strain into a copper mug or tumbler filled with ice.

(2) Top carefully with the chilled champagne.

Optional: garnish with candied ginger or honeycomb.

*Note: This recipe is also fantastic with gin in place of vodka. If you're a fan of whiskey, try it with bourbon, as in a **Kentucky Mule**. With rum, it's basically a Dark and Stormy—a **Champagne Dark and Stormy**. Catch my drift? You can sub almost any spirit in here and it will be delicious in an entirely new way.*

WATERMELON CAMPARI FIZZ

Tasting notes: bitter, bracing, juicy, refreshing

Campari's tangy rhubarb and bright orange notes make it a surprisingly good match for juicy watermelon in this luscious summer fizz. The liqueur's bracing bitterness is on full display, tempered by the rich body of Coco Lopez and the bright acidity of champagne and lime. It is beach weather incarnate.

YIELD: 1 COCKTAIL

1 ounce gin

1 ounce Campari

1 ounce fresh watermelon juice (page 122)

½ ounce fresh, strained lime juice

½ ounce Coco Lopez cream of coconut

Chilled champagne, to top (about 1 ounce)

Optional: watermelon ice cubes (page 122), to garnish

(1) Combine the gin, Campari, watermelon juice, lime juice, and Coco Lopez in a cocktail shaker filled with ice. Shake hard for 15 seconds, then strain into a chilled champagne glass *or* chilled rocks glass filled with ice.

(2) Top carefully with the chilled champagne.

Optional: garnish with watermelon cubes.

Note: *Campari cocktails have an almost magical ability to handle differing dilutions, so this one can be enjoyed either up or on the rocks. If you like the iced version, you can even try adding a splash of soda water or more watermelon juice to taste—it really is amazing how much variation this drink can handle.*

Note: *Coco Lopez is the most widely found brand of cream of coconut—it's in most grocery stores, often near the mixers. Sugar levels vary widely from brand to brand, so be aware of that if you use a different product; adjust the recipe accordingly.*

HONEYSUCKLE FIZZ

Tasting notes: an effervescent daiquiri with rich honey backbone

Honey transforms a basic Daiquiri into a Honeysuckle, and champagne transforms a Honeysuckle into a crisp, complex fizz. The richness and body of the honey bolsters the clean, nuanced flavors of the white rum so that they both shine—a true partnership.

YIELD: 1 COCKTAIL

**2 ounces white rum
(such as Flor de Caña)**

¾ ounce Honey Syrup (page 164)

½ ounce fresh, strained lime juice

**Chilled champagne, to top
(about 1 ounce)**

**Optional: lime wheel and dianthus
(as pictured) or other edible
flower, to garnish**

(1) Combine the rum, honey syrup, and lime juice in a cocktail shaker filled with ice. Shake hard for 15 seconds, then strain into a chilled champagne glass.

(2) Top carefully with the chilled champagne.

Optional: garnish with a lime wheel or edible flower.

Note: Though there aren't any actual honeysuckles in this cocktail, an edible flower garnish makes a fun and fragrant play on the drink's name and emphasizes the very light floral notes of a clean white rum. I like to pull the flower through a lime wheel (this is easier if you make a small X shape with a paring knife in the center), then carefully skewer the whole thing and balance it on the side of the glass. It can also be floated on top of the drink if the skewer proves too cumbersome, but you'll lose carbonation faster that way.

APPENDICES

Rosemary Chartreuse Spritz (page 58)

DRINKS BY SPIRIT & RECOMMENDED BOTTLES

In most cases, the best bottle to use is the one already on your shelf (if it's there, I'm assuming you already like it). If you find yourself in a position to restock, here are the exact bottles I used in the writing and testing of this book, plus their cost in my home state at the time of publication, and every cocktail in the book that uses them (so you can try other recipes with the leftovers). I know what it's like to run out to the liquor store for an ingredient, only to find when I get there that the ingredient is wildly expensive—and I want you to know exactly how pricey green Chartreuse is before you decide to give those recipes a try.

I've noted within certain recipes (the Scandi 75, for example) when a certain brand is necessary or highly preferred, because the flavor is too specific to be substituted without changes. I'm not being paid to promote any of these brands—I picked them all according to taste.

GIN

Plymouth Gin ($31.99 for 750 milliliters)
French 75, page 32
Rhubarb 75, page 146
Watermelon Campari Fizz, page 150
Pimm's Punch, page 70
Garden Party Punch, page 74
Persimmon Punch, page 78
Spiced Grapefruit Punch, page 86
Pimm's Royale, page 98
In Conclusion, page 130

COGNAC

Pierre Ferrand Ambre Cognac ($44.99 for 750 milliliters)
Champagne Sidecar, page 42
Chicago Cocktail, page 34
Ritz Cocktail, page 46
Chatham Artillery Punch, page 84
Three Acre Punch, page 87

RUM

Flor de Caña 4 Year Extra Seco White Rum ($12.79 for 750 milliliters)
Honeysuckle Fizz, page 152

Appleton Estate Signature Rum ($19.99 for 750 milliliters)
Airmail, page 45
Holiday Mail, page 140
Chatham Artillery Punch, page 84
Three Acre Punch, page 87
Grove Appeal, page 123

AQUAVIT

Krogstad Aquavit ($26.29 for 750 milliliters)
Scandi 75, page 136
Spiced Pear Punch, page 82

TEQUILA

Siembra Azul Blanco Tequila ($47.99 for 750 milliliters)
Spiced Tequila Tonic Sour, page 144
Spicy Blood Orange Serrano Mimosa, page 100
Margarita Fizz, page 126
Paloma Punch, page 72

VODKA

Tito's Handmade Vodka ($19.99 for 750 milliliters)
Watermelon Coconut Cooler, page 120
Honey Ginger Champagne Mule, page 148
Russian Spring Punch, page 76
Bubbly Mary, page 92
Melon Mint Mimosa, page 110

WHISKEY

Elijah Craig Small Batch Bourbon ($28.99 for 750 milliliters)
Boothby Cocktail, page 44
Seelbach, page 35
Chatham Artillery Punch, page 84

Old Overholt Straight Rye Whiskey ($19.99 for 750 milliliters)
Prince of Wales, page 36

Famous Grouse Scotch Whisky ($19.99 for 750 milliliters)
Spiced Scotch Pineapple Fizz, page 138

LIQUEURS

Luxardo Maraschino Liqueur ($29.99 for 750 milliliters)
Prince of Wales, page 36
Ritz Cocktail, page 46
In Conclusion, page 130

Clear Creek Distillery Cassis Liqueur ($19.99 for 375 milliliters)
Kir Royale, page 40
Russian Spring Punch, page 76

Aperol Aperitivo ($24.99 for 750 milliliters)
Aperol Spritz, page 57
Strawberry Tarragon Spritz, page 54
Persimmon Punch, page 78
Spicy Blood Orange Serrano Mimosa, page 100
Sole Rosso, page 114

Campari Bitter Aperitivo ($29.99 for 750 milliliters)
Campari Spritz, page 52
Strawberry Tarragon Spritz, page 54
Negroni Sbagliato, page 38
Watermelon Campari Fizz, page 150

Grand Marnier Liqueur ($34.99 for 750 milliliters)
Champagne Sidecar, page 42
Chicago Cocktail, page 34
Ritz Cocktail, page 46
Moonwalk, page 48
Seelbach, page 35
Sherry Spritz, page 53
Three Acre Punch, page 87
Mimosa, page 95
Apple Cider Mimosa, page 102
Strawberry Thai Basil Fizz, page 112
Orange Blossom, page 118
Grove Appeal, page 123
Margarita Fizz, page 126

St-Germain Elderflower Liqueur ($34.99 for 750 milliliters)
Strawberry Tarragon Spritz, page 54
Elderflower Spritz, page 62
Garden Party Punch, page 74
Elderflower Grapefruit Mimosa, page 96

Green Chartreuse Liqueur ($55.99 for 750 milliliters)
Rosemary Chartreuse Spritz, page 58
In Conclusion, page 130

Pimm's Cup No. 1 Liqueur ($19.99 for 750 milliliters)
Pimm's Royale, page 98
Pimm's Punch, page 70

FORTIFIED WINE

*Emilio Lustau Los Arcos Dry Amontillado Sherry
($19.99 for 750 milliliters)*
Sherry Spritz, page 53
Spiced Pear Punch, page 82
Bitter Sherry Fizz, page 132

Lillet Rose ($17.99 for 750 milliliters)
Strawberry Tarragon Spritz, page 54
Lillet Spritz, page 66

Dolin Blanc Vermouth de Chambery ($15.99 for 750 milliliters)
Vermouth Spritz, page 64

Carpano Antica Sweet Vermouth ($17.99 for 375 milliliters)
Negroni Sbagliato, page 38
Boothby Cocktail, page 44
Vermouth Spritz, page 64
Spiced Grapefruit Punch, page 86

FOUR BOTTLES,
EIGHTEEN COCKTAILS

If you only buy the gin, the St-Germain, the Grand Marnier, and the Aperol, you can make all of these drinks (with some grocery store items, too, of course):

DRINKS BY SEASON

Any cocktail in this book can be enjoyed year-round (save a few truly seasonal ingredients, like rhubarb and persimmon). But if you gravitate towards seasonality in your cocktail choices, here are some that best capture each time of year.

SPRING

SUMMER

WINTER

FALL

SYRUP RECIPES

SIMPLE SYRUP

So easy it shouldn't qualify as a recipe. Combine equal parts (ideally by weight, using a kitchen scale) sugar and water in a blender, then blend on high until the sugar is completely dissolved. With refrigeration, this syrup will stay fresh for about 2 weeks.

HONEY SYRUP

The best—dare I say only?—way to make a proper honey syrup is to weigh the ingredients, since honey is much denser than water. If you don't have a kitchen scale, get one! But in the meantime, the cheater measurements below will work in a pinch. This syrup will stay fresh with refrigeration for about 2 weeks.

YIELD: ABOUT 8 OUNCES

Measure out 128 grams (or, in a pinch, $^1/_3$ cup) very hot water and 200 grams (or, in a pinch, $^2/_3$ cup) honey. Stir or shake in a sealed container rapidly until completely combined. Store in the fridge.

CINNAMON SYRUP

This syrup is adapted from the recipe found in *Death & Co: Modern Classic Cocktails* by David Kaplan, Nick Fauchald, and Alex Day. If I'm not using it to liven up a cocktail (pair it with grapefruit or pineapple and prepare to be amazed), I'm using it to sweeten my morning coffee or a cup of black tea. It will stay fresh with refrigeration for about 2 weeks.

YIELD: ABOUT 2 CUPS

Break up 3 standard cinnamon sticks (about 3 inches long) in the bottom of a sturdy saucepan until they are smallish shards (a wooden mallet or muddler works well for this). Add 1 cup of water and 1 cup of sugar. Bring to a boil, stirring occasionally, then lower heat and simmer, covered, for 5 minutes. Remove from heat and let stand, still covered, at room temperature overnight. Strain through a fine mesh sieve and use immediately or store in the fridge.

GINGER HONEY SYRUP

This syrup, a staple in many bars and most notably used in the modern classic Penicillin, will stay fresh with refrigeration for about 2 weeks. Drizzle leftovers over ice cream or cake, or add them to plain seltzer for a stomach soother far superior to commercial ginger ale.

YIELD: ABOUT 10 OUNCES

Combine ¾ cup honey, ¾ cup water, and 1 large knot of ginger (about 6 inches long or 50 grams by weight, peeled and thinly sliced) in a saucepan over medium-high heat.

Bring to a boil, stirring occasionally, then reduce heat to low and let simmer 5 minutes. Remove from heat, cover, and let cool to room temperature. Refrigerate overnight (or at least 8 hours), then strain through a fine mesh sieve, discarding solids. Use immediately or store in the fridge.

RHUBARB SYRUP

Perhaps my all-time favorite seasonal syrup, this versatile recipe pairs the bright tanginess of rhubarb with warm vanilla and floral orange blossom to great effect. As a bonus, the leftover rhubarb pulp can be used as a compote—I love it on crostini with goat cheese, over vanilla ice cream, or showcased on a cheese plate.

YIELD: ABOUT 14 OUNCES

Combine ¾ pound chopped rhubarb in a saucepan with 1 cup water, 1 cup cane sugar, and 1 vanilla bean, split lengthwise. Bring to a boil over medium-high heat, stirring occasionally, then lower heat and cover. Let simmer gently for 5 minutes, then remove from heat.

Stir in ¼ teaspoon orange blossom water, replace lid, and let cool to room temperature. Refrigerate overnight (or at least 8 hours), then strain through a fine mesh sieve. Reserve the strained, broken-down rhubarb for use as a compote, and store both syrup and compote in the fridge.

RESOURCES

EDIBLE FLOWERS: If you don't grow them yourself, edible flowers can be incredibly hard to find. In the spring and summer, they tend to pop up in Whole Foods and other specialty food stores in the produce section, usually with the herbs. All of the flowers used in this book were purchased online (in the dead of winter, no less) from Gourmet Sweet Botanicals. The required overnight shipping isn't cheap, but the blooms themselves are very reasonable. The leaves and flowers I chose for these recipes came in packs of 50, and only cost between $10 and $15 per pack, making them a worthwhile party expense.

gourmetsweetbotanicals.com

GLASSWARE: Your local thrift store has all the vintage glassware you need, at a quarter of the price of an antique store—sometimes, for just a quarter. As someone who lives dangerously close to an antique store mecca and frequently makes antique purchases in other categories, I'm always blown away by how much easier it is to find the glassware I'm looking for in a thrift store. Most of the glasses in this book were purchased at my local thrift store for under a dollar apiece. The rest were purchased at Crate and Barrel (Edge Champagne Glass, Tour Double Old-Fashioned Glass), Anthropologie (Thalia Flute, Lottie Flute, Waterfall Stemless Wine Glass), and Sagaform (Gold Club Cocktail Glass).

BARWARE: If you need the basics—shakers, strainers, muddlers, spoons—head to Cocktail Kingdom. There's a reason this manufacturer and distributor of professional barware gets a shout-out in every modern cocktail book: they're simply the best. Nothing you buy here will be wrong—there's a wealth of knowledge in every design. Take, for example, the cocktail picks featured throughout this book. The flat, circular shape at the end isn't there just for looks—it actually makes balancing a garnish easier by preventing the pick from spinning.

cocktailkingdom.com

BOOKS: My library of cocktail-related books is, unsurprisingly, large—I owe a huge debt to the innovators and bartenders willing to be so generous with their knowledge. The titles that relate most closely to the subjects in this book are:

Uncorked: The Science of Champagne by Gérard Liger-Belair. As the title implies, this book has a wealth of information on the science behind champagne's character and behavior—it's the "why" behind many of the tips and practices I used in developing these recipes.

Champagne: The Essential Guide to the Wines, Producers, and Terroirs of the Iconic Region by Peter Liem. Interesting, informative guide to capital "C" Champagne (not the kind you should be pouring into these cocktails), with intimate, firsthand knowledge of the Champagne region and its winemakers as they stand today.

Liquid Intelligence: The Art and Science of the Perfect Cocktail by Dave Arnold. Simply put, my cocktail bible. If you want to learn the science behind all the myriad details that make up a perfectly mixed drink, plus many of Arnold's most approachable innovations based on these principles, you need this book in your library. Even though I've read it more than once, I still reference it almost daily.

ACKNOWLEDGMENTS

This book would not be possible without the people who have welcomed me into the moments in life most worthy of a good drink. To the friends, family, and colleagues who have perched with me on barstools and porch swings, wandered into gardens and across continents, and stayed up late because the conversation's just too good to end, the philosophy that drives my work is driven by you.

To my partner, Pat, I am most indebted for the completion of this book. Your confidence in it and in me was the single most important factor in getting it out of my head and onto paper. Thank you for handing over so much of your time and your palate without a second thought—for reading and rereading drafts, tasting and retasting recipes, and weighing in on every edit of every image. For coauthoring my life I'm especially grateful.

Kelly, my sister, for letting my copy you always, and for sharing your people with me. Thank you for doing everything first—and doing it so well.

Em, Jack, Mar, and Gabs, you are as much a part of this book as you are a part of me. As cheerleaders, coconspirators, guides, sounding boards, and release valves, you've never made me more grateful for the patient friendship of such impressive women. Laughing with you has been the privilege of a lifetime.

Mom and Dad, Jim and Laura, I've never taken a second of your boundless support and enthusiasm for granted. We all know I'm lucky to have you, especially me.

For the siblings and cousins and aunts and uncles I'm proud to call my friends and most willing guinea pigs—Joey, Matt, Sarah, Tim,

Andrew, Jon, and everyone else—family is the club I'm most grateful to belong to.

To the entire Murphy household, party to more than one punch debacle, never lose your fun.

Ludo, for sleeping on the kitchen floor instead of your bed so I wouldn't be alone as I worked into the wee hours, and for dragging me into the sunshine for walks when I couldn't possibly spare the time. You're my dog for the ages. I love you, good boy.

Finally, *Bubbly* would never have been realized without the superhuman patience and thoughtful guiding hand of Margaret McGuire Novak, my editor, or the passionate encouragement of my publisher John Whalen and Whalen Book Works. Special thanks to rockstar designer Melissa Gerber, proofreader Rebekah Slonim, and everyone else who made this book a reality.

And to you, for making my recipes and letting me into your life's good drink moments—my highest thanks will always be for you.

ABOUT THE AUTHOR
& PHOTOGRAPHER

Colleen Jeffers is a craft cocktail writer and photographer based in Bucks County, Pennsylvania. In 2015, she founded the Good Drink brand to make home bartending approachable for anyone with a passion for quality cocktails and a willingness to learn, no matter their skill level. *Bubbly* is her first book. For more of her writing and recipes, visit the @colljeffers Instagram feed or thegooddrink.com.

@colljeffers

INDEX

*Recipes in the book are in italics
(recipe variations are bolded).*

ABOUT WHALEN BOOK WORKS

PUBLISHING PRACTICAL & CREATIVE NONFICTION

Whalen Book Works is a small, independent book publishing company based in Kennebunkport, Maine, that combines top-notch design, unique formats, and fresh content to create truly innovative gift books.

Our unconventional approach to bookmaking is a close-knit, creative, and collaborative process among authors, artists, designers, editors, and booksellers. We publish a small, carefully curated list each season, and we take the time to make each book exactly what it needs to be.

We believe in giving back. That's why we plant one tree for every 10 books we print. Your purchase supports a tree in the Rocky Mountain National Park.

Get in touch!

Visit us at **whalenbooks.com**
or write to us at
68 North Street, Kennebunkport, ME 04046.